KINGS OF COMMERCE

Fr. GEORGE EASTMAN

KINGS OF COMMERCE

BY

T. C. BRIDGES

AND

H. HESSELL TILTMAN

WITH TWENTY-NINE ILLUSTRATIONS
IN HALF-TONE

Essay Index Reprint Series

BOOKS FOR LIBRARIES PRESS
FREEPORT, NEW YORK

First Published 1928
Reprinted 1968

LIBRARY OF CONGRESS CATALOG CARD NUMBER:
68-8442

PRINTED IN THE UNITED STATES OF AMERICA

FOREWORD

SUCCESS, the success which comes through taking risks and winning through, is always inspiring. In this volume will be found the stories of twenty-five famous British and American business-men who have achieved this kind of success. Most of them knew poverty before they became rich. Some, like Mr A. W. Gamage, Sir Thomas Lipton, and Mr Henry Ford, had no advantages whatever in the way of education, money, or friends to start them as boys on their upward careers.

The Old-World term for a company of men who sought new outlets for trade was 'merchant adventurers,' and all those whose stories are told here may justly be called adventurers, for their careers reveal the dogged persistence, energy, and courage which are the hall-mark of the pioneer. Some of us work for money, some for fame. These men have achieved both wealth and fame and—better than either—the respect and affection of their fellow-men. If you wish proof of this, you have it in the fact that the great businesses built up by these kings of commerce have been remarkably free from the strikes and labour troubles which have been the bane of business during the present century. While it is true that honesty is the best policy, kindness and consideration toward employees comes a good second.

These chapters, containing the lives of some of the most remarkable men of our time, are as thrilling as any tales of adventure, and it is the hope of the authors that a study of their pages will assist those in search of a career to decide on a vocation in life.

For the boys whose stories are written here are alike in only one thing. What they did they did better than ever was done before, and so readers will find not only interest but guidance and perhaps inspiration to win success for themselves.

H. HESSELL TILTMAN

T. C. BRIDGES

CONTENTS

ILLUSTRATIONS

KINGS OF COMMERCE

CHAPTER I

"DO YOUR JOB THE BEST YOU KNOW HOW"

The Story of Lord Ashfield

I HAVE often thought," says Lord Ashfield, with a twinkle in his eyes, " how very narrowly I missed becoming a minister of the Gospel instead of a Minister in the British Cabinet." In his early days Lord Ashfield was choir-boy in a famous church in the great American city of Detroit, and his parents were very desirous that he should go to college and be trained for the ministry.

Albert Henry Stanley, as he was then, had no such ambitions. His ideas ran not to surplices and pulpits, but to uniforms with brass buttons. He was oddly fascinated with the jingling horse-trams that ran past his house, and would spend many a spare minute gazing at them as they bumped along, packed with the passengers of the rapidly growing city. It seemed to him that rapid transit was the life of the town, and visions came to him of methods faster than trotting horses.

Since no one else sympathized with his ambitions he resolved to see what he could do on his own account, and one day took himself off to his clergyman, the Rev. John Munday. Mr Munday was an Englishman like himself, for be it remembered that Albert Stanley is British by birth as well as parentage, having been born in the ancient town of Derby in the year 1875. Boldly

Albert informed Mr Munday what he wanted to do, and asked him for a letter of introduction to the Scotsman who managed the tramways. Mr Munday hesitated, but, seeing how very much in earnest the boy was, at last gave him the note.

Albert, aged fourteen, a long, thin, eager lad, hurried off to the tram manager, and with the aid of his introduction 'landed' a job. "I think," he has since said, "that there was a conspiracy among them all to give me the hardest job they could, so that I should get tired of it and go back to school. I was put on as office- and odd-job boy in a small sub-office on the far side of the town. It meant getting up at six o'clock every morning, travelling right across the city, and beginning work at 7.30. Usually I was kept hard at it till ten at night."

Pretty stiff hours for a boy of fourteen, but not too much for young Albert Stanley, for work you like is almost as good as play, and the more he was given to do the more quickly he learned to do it. As for his pay, that was five dollars (£1) a week, and he not only lived on his wages, but saved enough to pay the fees for a spare-time course at a technical institute. It was fine training, for the boy came into touch with all grades, from managers and foremen to drivers, conductors, and rail-layers. He made himself familiar with every side of the work, and when the change came to electric traction was ready and prepared for it.

Detroit was one of the first cities in the United States to adopt electric traction for her tram system, and Stanley was so keen about it that he gave up his clerical work in order to take a job in the shops and so learn the technical and mechanical side of electricity. He went through every department, and in the evenings,

LORD ASHFIELD AND HIS DAUGHTER 14

After driving the first train at the reopening of the reconstructed City and South London Tube.

Photo L. N. A.

when the day's work was over, got one or other of the skilled mechanics to give him a little coaching and a few hints.

Good work usually meets with its reward, and when Stanley was eighteen he was given the important task of preparing the time- and journey-schedule for one of the tramway divisions. Then for the first time in his four years' work he struck serious trouble. A trade-union leader had been stirring up strife among the men employed by the Company, and by way of muzzling him the manager tried the experiment of putting him in charge of this particular division. To this man, as superintendent, Stanley brought his carefully prepared schedule. The fellow glanced through it and went red with rage. "You don't reckon my men is going to stand for hours like these?" he roared. "Take it away." He said a lot more, but his remarks would not look well in cold print. Then, seizing young Stanley, he shoved him out of the office.

It was a deadlock; the men became threatening; but just then the agitator was taken ill and had to go to hospital.

The manager sent for Stanley. "What's to be done? The men won't work to your schedule."

"I can make them," said Stanley. "Let me run the line."

"You—a mere boy! You're crazy."

"I can do the job. Give me the chance," begged Stanley; and the other, impressed by his intense earnestness, told him he could try. He tried, he succeeded, the trade-union leader never came back, and Stanley kept his job. 'Some job' too, for that winter Detroit was visited by one snowstorm after another and by alternate frosts and thaws. Masses of ice formed in the streets, covering the rails and forcing the cars off the track. The young superintendent spent half his time out in the open, often helping with his own hands to get cars back on the rails.

Perhaps because he was never afraid of tucking up his sleeves and tackling any sort of job Stanley was very popular with his men, and one Christmas had a pleasant surprise in the shape of a rifle presented to him by the drivers and conductors of his section. The manager was as interested in the new rifle as its owner, and the two took it out on Christmas morning to try it. The manager had just shot at a target pinned on a fence when some one called out, "The police are coming. Better put that rifle away." So Stanley and his boss hurried into the office and hid the rifle. In strode the superintendent of police in a rare rage. Pulling off his helmet, he showed the horrified culprits a hole through the top of it. A bullet ricochetting from the fence had missed his head by an uncomfortably narrow margin. There was a terrible fuss, and the manager was told that the culprit must be dismissed. However, as Lord Ashfield says, the manager did not feel like dismissing himself, and in the end the awkward incident was smoothed over.

Another story Lord Ashfield tells relates to an early attempt on his part to advertise his trams. There was at that time an Indian reservation near Detroit, and the trams ran through it. He got the idea of getting one of the Indian chiefs to carry a sandwich-board, wearing his full war-paint. The chief was quite keen, but stipulated that he must have a free pass on the trams, and this was granted. Then trouble started, for the old Indian spent his entire time riding up and down on trams. It did not matter what the weather was, there he sat, proud as a peacock, rumbling up and down the steel rails. The white passengers did not like it. They said he did not wash—that they did not like the smell of him. Complaints rolled in faster and faster. "A nice job I had to get that pass back from him," said Lord Ashfield. "But I did it at last, and peace reigned once more."

Young Stanley's rapid rise continued, and at twenty—an age when most boys are just starting in business—he was actually managing the whole tramway system of Detroit and the surrounding country with a salary of 5000 dollars (£1000) a year. Detroit was growing very fast at this time, and Stanley took care that its transport system grew with it. He kept on running out fresh lines, until there were no fewer than 550 miles of track. Most young men would have been well satisfied with such a position, but Stanley was looking for bigger opportunities. He carefully followed tramway developments in other parts of the country, and kept in touch with all the important people interested in these movements. In 1903 he heard that a big scheme was afoot to amalgamate the urban traction of the state of New Jersey, and, acting with his usual promptness, he applied for the managership. He got it, and at twenty-eight was head of the whole huge business, running nearly 1000 miles of electric railway, with 25,000 men under him, and a salary of 15,000 dollars (£3000).

Previous to this he had had an interesting experience. When the trouble with Spain began in 1898 he had joined the naval reserve, with the result that when war broke out between the two countries he was drafted into the Navy and sent as an ordinary seaman to the *Yosemite*, a merchant vessel which had been transformed into an auxiliary cruiser and carried the first load of guns to Cuba. The *Yosemite* got mixed up in the mine-fields, and on more than one occasion was in great danger, owing to mines getting entangled with the propellers. "Our job then," says Lord Ashfield, "was to strip and go overboard to disentangle them." Later he helped to capture a Spanish warship off Porto Rico, and had a share in the prize-money.

Now we come to the events which brought Stanley back to the country of his birth. London's first Underground Railway was opened so long ago as 1863, and had been gradually extended, first into a complete inner circle, then into an outer circle. But the trains were pulled by old-fashioned steam locomotives, and the atmosphere of the tunnels was horrible. It was particularly bad on the northern side of the Inner Circle, and between Gower Street and King's Cross the air was sometimes almost unbreathable. Also everything, including the carriages, was black with soot and smoke. Passengers grew heartily sick of it, and in 1904 electrification began. A group of American financiers, including the late Mr Yerkes, was interested in the electrification, and much of the new machinery was being imported from America. A Boston firm who were deeply engaged, and perhaps rather alarmed, about the prospects of London's Underground decided that Albert Stanley was the best man to send over to look after their affairs. Stanley himself was none too keen on the suggestion, and though in the end he agreed, he stipulated that his engagement was to be for a year only, at the end of which time he was to be free to return to America. Certainly at that time he never dreamed of what the future held in store for him.

When he arrived in London he found things in a bad way. The Underground system was not only unable to pay interest on its ordinary shares, but even on its debentures. It was, in fact, on the very edge of bankruptcy. Mr Stanley called a meeting of all the officials and told them just how matters stood. "I have," he said, "persuaded the banks to advance £50,000 for the purpose of advertising the Underground, and I mean to do that vigorously for six months. Meantime I am going to ask you all to hand in your resignations—to take effect in six months if we cannot make good." One and all agreed, and then dispersed to meet again in six months.

Mr Stanley's next move was to make a tour of the newspaper offices and tell the editors the exact position. The editors said, "If you have any developments to report, that is news, and we will print it." Developments began at once, the papers printed the stories, and there was no need to use the £50,000. At the end of the six months the new manager was able to tell his officers that he was not going to ask for any resignations—that the future was safe. Then began the amalgamation of the various London Tubes, bus-companies, and trams, and year by year the business has increased, until in 1927 the passengers carried by the group numbered 1,669,000,000 in addition to 604,000,000 carried by associated companies. Traffic receipts amounted to nearly fourteen millions sterling. The staff numbered about 40,000, with an average weekly wage of £4 2*s.* 10*d.* More than one and a quarter millions were spent on Underground stations, and nearly seven hundred thousand on omnibus improvement. Within the last few years more than six millions have been spent in driving new lines and improving old ones, and the improvements originated by its chief have made London's Tubes an example to the rest of the world. Escalators, passimeters, roll-tick machines for ticket-issuing—all these and many other improvements were first adopted on London's Underground system. Another interesting point is that Underground coaches were the first to be built of fireproofed wood.

In 1914 Mr Stanley received the well-deserved reward of a knighthood, and it is said that this was the first year in which he ever took a real holiday. Pretty nearly a record, one would fancy, for he was then thirty-nine years of age, and had been hard at work for a quarter of a century. This holiday nearly landed him into serious trouble, for on August 1, four days before the Great War broke out, he was in Baden. Some one gave him a quiet hint that it might be well to be moving, but when he went to the station he was refused a ticket. He wasted no time in buying a car and hurrying off, but before he reached the frontier his car was stopped and confiscated. Somehow he smuggled himself aboard a train loaded with soldiers, and so reached Holland. He landed in London the very night before war was declared.

Having offered his services to the State, he was at once given an important post managing motor transport under the Ministry of Munitions, and did this so well that in less than two years he was made President of the Board of Trade. Here he was in command of practically the whole railway system of Great Britain, a mighty big job, but not one that anyone need have envied him. One of the first things he was forced to do was to put up railway fares by 50 per cent., which did not make the public bless him, and the next to cut down the ordinary passenger-service of the country by about half, a still more unpopular proceeding. But it was the only way in which to get engines and rolling stock and steel rails to take the allied troops to the Front in France. Both the country of his birth and that of his adoption owe him much for what he did in the war, and no peerage was better earned than that which was given him in the year 1920.

Do not think that because he has worked so hard all his life Lord Ashfield is therefore unable to enjoy himself. You need only look at his photograph to see that he is very human and has a keen sense of humour. His chief recreation is golf, and his pet aversion is making a speech.

CHAPTER II

AN EMIGRANT BOY WHO "MADE GOOD"

Edward Bok, a Modern Pioneer

LORD NORTHCLIFFE once told one of the present writers that there was one story he would, had he the power, place in the hands of every young man on the threshold of life's adventures. It was the story of a little Dutch immigrant to the United States, whose first job brought him fifty cents a week, and who made himself one of America's greatest journalists. Here is the story, some of the details of which have been taken from the autobiography written by Edward Bok, the little Dutch boy, and to which Lord Northcliffe wrote an introduction (*Edward Bok: An Autobiography*, published by Thornton Butterworth).

The Bok family arrived at New York in 1870. There were six of them—father, mother, and four children. The family had been well off, but unwise investments had swept away their fortune, and so the father had decided to make a new start in a new land rather than live in poverty at home.

Edward Bok, the boy of whom this chapter tells, was then a lad of seven years. Early in life Edward and his elder brother found themselves facing its problems, for their father found it difficult to adapt himself to the new land, and their mother, forced to run the little home without any domestic help, and often with very little food, found the task almost beyond her powers. To help her the two boys rose early in the morning, lit the fire, prepared breakfast, and washed the dishes before going to school. In the evenings, when their schoolmates were playing, they returned home and worked in the house until bedtime. It was hard on two boisterous boys, but this early experience of running a home was to prove useful to Edward Bok in a way he little expected.

Housework lightened his mother's burden, but little Bok soon realized that more than that was needed—money, the power to earn was what was lacking in their home. He thought this over. Probably he was thinking of it when one day he looked into the windows of a baker's shop and noticed that they needed cleaning.

That was his first idea, and he acted upon it. Into the shop he went and offered to clean them. The baker accepted the offer, and, impressed by the energy by which the boy set about the task, he engaged him there and then to clean the windows twice a week for a wage of fifty cents.

It was a beginning, but half a dollar a week did not appeal to Edward Bok as exactly a princely salary, so he still kept his eyes open. One day, waiting in the shop after cleaning the windows, he served a customer in the baker's absence. His employer returned in time to see the smart way he wrapped up the cakes, and thereupon offered him a dollar a week extra to sell behind the counter in the afternoons.

He agreed to come in on all afternoons except Saturday. He had two more ideas calculated to be worth money for that day. The first was a newspaper delivery in the morning (there was no school on Saturday), which brought his wages up to two and a half dollars. For the afternoon he had an idea which shows clearly that touch of imagination which was eventually destined to bring him fame from one end of America to the other.

In Brooklyn, where he then lived, the people travelled in from outlying districts in horse-trams, and the horses were watered close to his home. Edward Bok's quick intellect had noted that in hot weather the people arrived thirsty, and were forced to wait for the horses and then ride on into Brooklyn before they could secure a drink of any sort. Here was yet another chance to earn more money for his mother—but the story is best told in his own words as he wrote it in his book *Edward Bok.*

> He bought a shining new pail, screwed three hooks on the edge from which he hung three clean, shimmering glasses, and one Saturday afternoon when a car stopped the boy leapt on, tactfully asked the conductor if he did not want a drink, and then proceeded to sell his water, cooled with ice, at one cent a glass to the passengers. A little experience showed that he exhausted a pail with every two trams, and each pail netted him thirty cents.
>
> But the profits of six dollars which Edward was now reaping in his newly found 'bonanza' on Saturday and Sunday afternoons became apparent to other boys, and one Saturday the young ice-water boy found that he had a competitor; then two and three. Edward immediately met the challenge; he squeezed half a dozen lemons into each pail of water, added some sugar, tripled his charge, and continued his monopoly by selling "Lemonade—three cents a glass." Soon more passengers were asking for lemonade than water.

Young Bok was now earning more than most boys of his age, but he wanted still more. It was not long before another idea presented itself to his fertile brain. He was asked to a party, and while there it occurred to him that all the guests would probably like to see their names in the local paper. So he wrote an account of the party, added the names of all those present, and offered it to the local editor. It was his first attempt at journalism, and it was bought and printed.

That editor, realizing that all those whose names appeared in his pages would buy one or two copies of the paper, asked Bok for more, and soon the boy was sending in numbers of reports, partly collected by himself and partly by his friends—but all paid for at the rate of four dollars per column.

All this was very exciting, but it left very little time in which to squeeze in school-lessons. For a term or two Edward Bok tried both to learn and earn. Finally he approached his father about a position for an office-boy in a telegraph company which he had heard was vacant, and asked permission to apply for the post.

Realizing how keen he was, and possibly also that a boy of his quick mind was likely to learn as much in the world as he would at school, Mr Bok, Senior, consented, and so at the age of thirteen Edward Bok said good-bye to schooldays and began the adventure of living.

Although he had left school he was sufficiently intelligent to understand that there were many things he must learn if he were to succeed. After careful thought he decided that the first thing to do was to study the lives of other famous men who had risen from small beginnings. In other words, he wanted to read a volume containing the stories of great men similar to the volume now in your hands, and by searching the local library he found it in a book called the *New American Cyclopædia.*

Having found the book he wanted, he began to save the money necessary to buy it by the simple expedient of cutting down his lunches and walking five miles to the office and five miles home each day instead of riding there. In a few weeks a copy of the encyclopædia was his, and he was heartened to find, as he had suspected, that many of the famous Americans whose life-romances were told in its pages had been just as poor as he was at one time.

The passion for self-education thus begun gave Bok his next great idea.

He had begun collecting autographs of famous people, writing to many of those in his encyclopædia and usually receiving letters in reply. These letters made the famous more interesting to him—some of them he actually interviewed in his quest for autographs—and he read every word about them that he could find.

Then one day he picked up a cigarette-card thrown down in the street. He looked at the picture of a famous actress, turned the card over, and found the other side blank. Now that was waste space—surely these cards would be more interesting to a public that liked scraps of useful knowledge if on the other side of the card they found a little hundred-word biography of the famous man or woman whose picture it was.

The next day he sought out the company that printed the cards and explained his idea. The manager saw the possibilities of the idea, and he ordered a set of one hundred little biographies on the spot at ten dollars apiece.

Here was real money at last. Joyously Bok settled down to write the biographies of men and women whose careers in most cases he already knew by heart. Hardly was the first set complete when the firm asked for a second hundred, and then a third.

To get them out in time Edward Bok offered his elder

brother a pound for each biography he would write. Later he made a similar offer to one or two local journalists whom he could trust to be accurate. Soon he had five writers busily hunting up facts about the great and turning in the little hundred-word biographies, while he 'edited' them and passed them on to the firm which was distributing this knowledge all over the country on the backs of cigarette-cards. Thus Edward Bok can claim to be the first and only famous journalist who got his start in journalism by editing cigarette-pictures!

His thoughts were now turning directly to journalism. Like many other boys who have once known the joys of seeing something they have laboriously written in print, he knew that no other career would satisfy him. But to get on in journalism you must know shorthand, so after leaving the telegraph office at night he went to two sets of shorthand classes. He learnt it in two places because he was in a hurry and the local business college only held two classes a week, whereas he was prepared to devote four evenings a week to the task.

Soon after he had completed his studies he got his first chance as a newspaper reporter when the editor of the local paper asked him to report two speeches—one by the President of the United States—which were to be delivered at a meeting in Brooklyn.

Young Bok went, and when he found that the President spoke too rapidly for his newly acquired shorthand to set all his phrases down he went to the great man at the end and, explaining how much success in this, his first reporting job, meant to him, asked him for a copy of the speech. Evidently the President was impressed by his enthusiasm, for Bok got a copy of the speech, and had the joy of finding that his paper was the only one to print the speech in full.

This astounding boy, who, as the reader will now probably agree with us, was undoubtedly marked out for brilliant success in journalism from birth, was now finding his feet. He seized the chance of a summer holiday to go to Boston, where he secured an interview with Oliver Wendell Holmes, the famous American author, who lived in that town. Later he went to the theatre with Longfellow, the author of *Hiawatha*. Another American literary 'giant' who consented to see the young man with a passion for meeting the great was Ralph Waldo Emerson, the world-famous essayist. The little Dutch immigrant boy was moving in high society with a vengeance.

When a little later he secured the editorship of a local church paper which had been rechristened the *Brooklyn Magazine* these friendships stood him in good stead, and his rivals wondered how Bok managed to get so many famous people to write for the paper.

The joy of editing this magazine in the evenings made his work as stenographer at the telegraph office in the daytime seem more and more monotonous, and eventually he made a determined effort to secure another position in the publishing world. Through his chief he got a post in the offices of a well-known New York firm of publishers.

The *Brooklyn Magazine*, which under his direction had attained a large sale, had attracted the attention of a wealthy man, who had purchased it in order to provide an occupation for his son, so Bok was left without a regular evening occupation. This did not fit in with his plans for two reasons. One was that his father had recently died, and Edward Bok and his brother were anxious to make enough to enable their mother to live in the comfort to which she had been accustomed before coming to America. The other reason was his belief that the man who could do two jobs got on twice as fast as the man who did one.

Looking around for an opening for his talents, he hit upon the idea, then almost unheard-of, of selling the same articles to a number of widely scattered papers for publication in all of them on the same day. This is called 'syndicating,' and it was an instant success.

Developing his latest idea, Bok opened offices in New York, and as he was engaged at the publisher's office all day made his brother William partner. From this office he sent out the first woman's page ever printed in the American newspapers.

The papers of those days paid little attention to women's interests, a fact which Bok's quick mind seized upon. He decided that he would pay particular attention to women's matters—and thereby he began his training for the biggest success of his life.

After two years with the publishing house he got the chance of a position as stenographer in the office of Scribner's, one of the most famous publishing firms in America. He took it, thereby raising his salary to nearly twenty dollars a week, apart from his earnings from the 'syndicate.'

When he joined Scribner's this born journalist was just twenty-one years of age. It seems impossible that any boy, however brilliant, could have achieved all that has been written in this chapter before reaching manhood, but such was Bok's capacity for hard work that he had done it.

Before long he was promoted, and left letter-writing behind him for advertising work. He enjoyed every minute of it, worked early and late, but he did not neglect his spare-time interests, among which was now a weekly book feature, which was appearing in forty-five papers.

That weekly book feature was responsible for Edward Bok's next move, and the one which gave him the real chance he had been waiting for. One of the papers which published it belonged to a Mr Curtis, the owner of the *Ladies' Home Journal,* who was looking for an editor. He read the weekly review and decided that the writer of it was the man he wanted. He came to New York and offered him the job.

For a few days Edward Bok hesitated. It was a big step. The *Ladies' Home Journal* was not then the great magazine which it is to-day. To become its editor meant leaving a sure position with a great publishing house and leaving New York—above all, leaving his mother. His friends advised him to refuse. Fortunately he did not refuse. Instead he bought copies of various other women's magazines, studied the opposition and the possibilities, and decided that he could make the *Ladies' Home Journal* a success. Having come to this conclusion, he resigned his position in New York and took the train for Philadelphia, the scene of his new work.

There is no need to write here of all the ideas which flowed from that ever-youthful brain into the *Ladies' Home Journal,* although for those interested in journalism there is romance in every one of them. Bok's great idea was to make the readers write to his staff of experts whenever they required information upon any subject of interest to women. For the thirty years during which

EDWARD BOK 30

Photo Sport and General

he retained that editorship he kept that plan in the very forefront of his programme. He had thirty-five associate editors on the staff, and the circulation rose to be the largest ever attained by a woman's journal in the world.

When the entry of the United States into the World War temporarily stopped this side of the paper's work the number of letters received in each year had reached one million!

What was the greatest lesson which the little Dutch boy learned during those thirty years of success? It was always to give more than was necessary for the salary he was getting at the moment.

In his book, *Edward Bok: An Autobiography*, he reminds the reader that he never worked by the clock, always by the job, and saw that it was well done regardless of the time it took to do it.

He took care never to live up to his income, and as his salary increased so he increased the percentage of it which he saved.

At forty years of age this remarkable man began to plan his own retirement, believing that it is better for a journalist to go while his paper is prosperous than to hang on until his public begins to tire of his ideas.

After the most successful career of any journalist of his generation he deliberately decided that he would hand over his work to a younger man when he reached the age of fifty.

As events turned out he was fifty-six, and had completed thirty strenuous years in the editorial chair, when at length he retired.

During those years he had seen the circulation of his paper grow under his direction from 440,000 copies a month to nearly two millions, and thus become the most valuable magazine property in the New World.

The story of Edward Bok is not just an ordinary story of success, it is a story which reveals how a penniless boy, without wealth, position, or friends—an exile in a foreign land—can, given a touch of genius and a capacity for hard work, make of his life a success held up for all men to copy.

And after talking with him one of the writers came to the conclusion that this was the fact about his life-story of which he was most proud.

It will be a long time before journalists either in Britain or America forget to point to this wonderful career when wishing to inspire their sons. His success as an editor has become almost a legend. But we think that, looking back over a remarkable life, it would be true to say that Edward Bok was never nearer to being a genius than on that Saturday afternoon in Brooklyn when, finding too many rivals competing with him in selling iced water to the tramcar passengers, he had his great ' brain wave ' and squeezed lemons into his bucket, thus recapturing his lost custom and beating his competitors.

That story of the youthful Bok is worth remembering. It is the tale of a pioneer who did not know the meaning of defeat.

CHAPTER III

"MONEY LOST, LITTLE LOST"

The Romance of Charles Cochran

CHARLES COCHRAN is an actor. You cannot possibly put him in a book of this sort," said a scandalized friend to the writer of this chapter. It is quite true that C. B. *was* an actor, and had the good sense to see that he would never make a fortune as such. He therefore turned himself into a showman, and if a showman is not a man of business, who is? Not merely a showman, but the greatest showman of the present century, and—what is better—the most popular, the kindest, and straightest of showmen.

Showmanship is the most risky business in existence, and Mr Cochran has had his ups and downs. The proof of his popularity is that when, at one period of his career, he went bankrupt he was almost swamped with letters containing cheques and banknotes from those whom he had befriended in the past, and before he could set about making a fresh fortune he had to spend days in returning these, each with a personal note of thanks.

One of a big family of ten, Charles Cochran lived as a boy in the Sussex village of Lindfield, and the first play he ever saw was the pantomime *Sinbad the Sailor* at the Theatre Royal, Brighton. Arthur Roberts was the chief comedian, and one sight of Arthur Roberts decided young Cochran that he too would be a comedian.

Meantime he had to go to school. He was sent to a school at Eastbourne, where he tells us that his main interest was in white mice and lizards, and that his conduct was disorderly: so disorderly that, after a bonfire rag one fifth of November, his head master expelled him. But there is nothing disgraceful about an expulsion of that sort, and he had no difficulty in entering Brighton Grammar School, where he shared a study with a thin, delicate-looking red-haired boy named Aubrey Beardsley, who later gained world-wide fame as a caricaturist.

There was a master who was keen on amateur theatricals, and almost every week a performance of some sort was given. One, *The Pied Piper*, was presented at the Dome, and the *Sussex Daily News* gave Cochran his first notice, saying that his work was quite professional.

At sixteen Cochran left his school. His father had lost money, and the boy went into a surveyor's office. He made friends with the manager of the Brighton Alhambra and a pianist named Wilson, and through the former had his first professional engagement, which was to sing comic songs at Dover. "It was," he says in his book, *Secrets of a Showman*,[1] "a complete failure. My turn finished with the first song, and the manager refused to pay me." It speaks well for young Cochran's pluck that his failure did not in the least discourage him.

That was in 1890. In December of that year a young artist named Scotson Clark whom Cochran had known at school suggested that they should try their fortune together in America. Cochran agreed, saved every penny, and finally had enough to pay for a steerage ticket to New York.

Herded at first with a lot of filthy Lithuanians, the

[1] London: Wm. Heinemann Ltd.

CHARLES B. COCHRAN AND SOME OF HIS YOUNG LADIES 34
Photo Sport and General

two boys were driven to sleep on deck, but some of the sailors were good to them and allowed them to sleep in the fo'c'sle while they themselves were on duty on deck.

They had not ten pounds between them when they landed in New York, and the thing was to get work, and get it quickly. They were taken on as 'supers' at the Star Theatre, but Cochran was ignominiously turned down by the producer, who grimly said he wanted ladies and gentlemen, *not* children. Scotson Clark was kept on at a dollar a performance, and with his help Cochran managed to exist until at last he was engaged to sing at Huber's Museum. Eight performances a day and thirty dollars a week. This did not last long, but a little later Cochran was engaged to play in *Our Boys*. It was a 'frost,' and Cochran had hard times before he got another job. Indeed, the soles were literally coming off his boots before he 'landed' one.

The next year was enough to have broken the spirit of any youngster less determined to get on than Charles Cochran. He was often hungry, and once had to sleep in a fifteen-cent lodging-house in Chicago, a place of the same sort as the fourpenny doss-houses of East London. He tried to join Barnum's Show, but was turned down by Imre Kiralfy, and was driven to join a travelling medicine show and sell pots of ointment for a living.

The turning-point came when he made the acquaintance of Richard Mansfield. Mansfield, though English-born, was at that time America's greatest actor, and held much the position in the States that Irving held in England. And Mansfield was good to the unknown youngster, laughed at the story of his experiences, and promised him a part in a new play. But there was a gap to fill in first, and Cochran's saved money was at an end. He went to the Y.M.C.A. and became assistant to the Church of England chaplain to the Port of New York. It meant boarding liners and interviewing new arrivals, and the pay was two dollars (8*s.*) a day. Cochran disliked it intensely and was glad to give it up and begin work with Mr Mansfield.

One day Mr Mansfield called Cochran into his private car—the company was on tour at the time—and said to him, " Do you think, Cochran, you will ever be a good actor ? "

Badly scared, Cochran assured Mr Mansfield that he was doing his best.

" I don't think you will ever be a great actor," said Mr Mansfield. " How would you like to be my secretary ? You shall have ten dollars a week extra and be my private secretary."

Mansfield was a difficult man to work for, yet on the whole Cochran got on well with him, and incidentally met many interesting people. But at last a split came, and Cochran, with Ted Henley, started a school of acting in New York. That did not last long, and Cochran returned to Mansfield for a while.

But he had been seven years in America and was anxious to see England again. He crossed on a tramp steamer of which the skipper was a Scottish Presbyterian. On the first Sunday out he found his passenger reading *Martin Chuzzlewit* and snatched the book. " Wud ye bring down the wrath of God on the vessel ? Reading novels on the Sabbath ? " he cried, and flung the book overboard.

It was pleasant to meet his father and old friends again, but Cochran found it terribly hard to get a footing in English theatrical circles. He took to writing theatrical articles for *The Critic* and other papers. Even then he was so hard up that at times he nearly starved, and was reduced to walking about the streets because he had not money to pay for a bed.

Luck turned again. Mr Mansfield arrived in London and asked Cochran to return with him to America, where he was going to produce *Cyrano*. For eight weeks the play packed the Garden Theatre in New York. People lined up thirty-six hours in advance to get seats. There were fights in the queue. One man was shot, another stabbed.

Cochran's ambition to work for himself and become a manager was as strong as ever. He told Mr Mansfield, who sent him to England to look for a suitable play. Back in London he met Ellaline Terriss and lunched with George Bernard Shaw. Then Mansfield cabled him to come back. He decided to remain in England and so began his career in London.

His first start was the management of a touring company; then he became agent for the well-known singer Templar Saxe, and was so successful with him that he started an office in Chancery Lane as a regular theatrical and music-hall agent.

The list of celebrities who have passed through Charles Cochran's hands is immense. One of the first was the late Houdini, the Handcuff King. Cochran took him to Germany, where Houdini terribly upset the German police by extricating himself from a Black Maria after he had been handcuffed with the regulation German police handcuffs. Another performance which amazed everybody was Houdini's being handcuffed and sealed in a sack which was flung into a river. " It was as tense a thrill as ever I experienced," said Mr Cochran. "It seemed many minutes before Houdini came to the surface, but he did come up, quite free, and swam to the bank."

Another of Mr Cochran's finds was Georges Hackenschmidt, the Russian wrestler. Hackenschmidt had appeared at the Tivoli, but without much success, and was bent on returning to Paris. Mr Cochran got him to come round to the Hotel Cecil, where he looked him over and was amazed at his magnificent physique. He says he was the finest specimen of humanity he ever saw.

Mr Cochrane went to Mr Payne, who controlled the Syndicate Halls, and got a contract for Hackenschmidt at £70 a week, and during that week the Tivoli, where Hackenschmidt was showing, broke the record for box-office receipts. As a result Hackenschmidt's salary was increased to £150 a week.

Mr Cochran knew that Lancashire was the home of wrestling and decided to take the Russian there. He took the Prince of Wales Theatre in Liverpool and had all arrangements made, when Mr Cleaver, the owner, became afraid that he might endanger his licence by allowing wrestling on the stage and notified Mr Cochran that he would not allow the performance. The latter sent out sandwichmen announcing that the contest would take place, and Cleaver sent out others declaring that it would not. Mr Cochran got possession of the theatre, and Hackenschmidt and the other wrestlers held it against all comers. Then the opposition cut off the gas, but an officer of the gas company who was keen on wrestling got that put right.

This was not the end, for at the very last minute the lights went out. Cleaver had cut the pipes. The friendly official hunted up gas-fitters, in less than half an hour the lights were ablaze, and the entertainment was given to a packed house.

Mr Cochran's solicitor warned him that he must give up possession of the house at midnight or be guilty of trespass, and that then he must endeavour to secure the house again next day. Next day the whole place was locked and barred. Mr Cochran broke a window and got in, but as soon as he was inside some one hit him over the head and some one else turned a hose on the rest of his party. He and his men stuck to it and got in, only to find that all the fittings had been removed. So the game was up and the " battle of Clayton Square " was over.

Hackenschmidt was taken to Manchester, where he was a huge success, then back to London, where he encountered Madrali, the Terrible Turk. Hackenschmidt was extremely nervous, but when the great contest at last began he " rushed at his opponent like a tiger, encircled his huge body with his arms, lifted him shoulder high, and threw him on the ground with a thud that sounded like a sack of potatoes falling."

Wrestlers arrived from all over the world, London went mad on wrestling, yet knew so little of the game that when a real contest took place—as between Pedersen and Aberg—the audience thought it was a fake and behaved so badly that the manager stopped the contest.

Hackenschmidt had a wonderful appetite. He came to dine one night at Mr Cochran's flat in Piccadilly, and Mrs Cochran provided quantities of food. He ate eight or nine eggs, a porterhouse steak, and a whole Camembert cheese. Mrs Cochran then asked if she could get him anything more, and Hackenschmidt smilingly replied,

"No, thanks. I have to dine with some friends, so I will not spoil my appetite."

Hackenschmidt went to Australia, and Mr Cochran got hold of Zbysco, a huge Austrian, who was as unpopular with the public as Hackenschmidt was the reverse. One of Zbysco's shows at the Pavilion upset the audience so much that they started to wreck the house. On this occasion Zbysco was wrestling with a big Turk named Kara Suliman, and the conditions were that Zbysco should pay the Turk a sum of money if he failed to throw him within ten minutes. He failed and refused to go on with the contest, but the audience yelled for a finish, and when Zbysco again refused they tore the electric-light fittings from the wall and hurled them on the stage.

One of the funniest happenings of that wrestling era was when a match was fixed between Zbysco and Suliman—two falls out of three—at the Holborn Empire.

Aware that Turkish wrestlers sometimes cover themselves with grease, Mr Cochran bargained that both contestants should have a warm bath in the theatre before taking the mat. The wrestlers hated the idea, but he insisted, and a firm of soap-manufacturers took the front page of the *Daily Mail* on the day of the match and had a picture showing the two men being rubbed down by Mr Cochran with their soap. Incidentally they paid Mr Cochran well for the use of their soap—which shows how good a man of business a showman may be.

It was Mr Cochran who coined the term 'Fun City' which has since become so familiar. His first Fun City was at Olympia, a sort of fair with roundabouts, coconut-shies, a menagerie, and a circus. One side-show which was very successful was Sacco, the Fasting Man, who spent fifty-two days in a sealed glasshouse on water only. Certain doctors objected to this show as "degrading and unwholesome," and a medical paper attacked the Exhibition. Finally Mr Cochran's partner said that it was to cease.

Mr Cochran saw his chance. "We have rented to Sacco the premises he is occupying," he answered, "and we might find ourselves involved in an action for illegal trespass if we turned him out." Mr Cochran's solicitor agreed. He said that Mr Cochran might serve Sacco with a notice to quit, but if he refused to do so the use of force would be at his risk.

So a letter was written, and all London became aware of what was about to happen. On a Saturday afternoon Mr Cochran walked up to Sacco's prison and placed against the window a notice that he must come out, or the door would be broken down.

Sacco wrote that he refused to move and would sue if interfered with. Mr Cochran turned to a boy who carried a hatchet. "Break down the door," he ordered.

A solicitor engaged by Sacco stepped up and threatened heavy damages, and Mr Cochran's own solicitor agreed. In the end Mr Cochran allowed himself to be persuaded. "Well," he said, "we have done our best. If the man wants to kill himself we cannot interfere."

It was a splendid advertisement. There was a rush to see Sacco. The entrance-fee was raised from sixpence to one shilling, then to two and sixpence, and, on the day he broke his fast, to five shillings.

In any business it is the man who can see farthest ahead who does best. The showman must be quickest of all to see the first signs of a change in the fashion of amusement and to be ready for it. London was getting tired of wrestlers and fasting men. In conversation with an American friend, Mr C. P. Crawford, Mr Cochran decided that it was about time for a new boom in roller-skating, and the result was that Olympia was fitted up as a rink. It was a success from the first minute. London went mad on 'rolling,' and the roller-skating mania spread all over the country much as greyhound-racing did in 1927.

Not satisfied with the profits to be made in England Mr Cochran became manager of rinks in Paris, Hamburg, Berlin, Antwerp, and Nice. The best rink was in Berlin, but the irony of it was that the road outside was so good that hundreds of people skated there instead of coming into the rink. The life of a well-conducted skating-rink is about three years, the longest-lasting being one of the two Parisian rinks, which lasted for four years. At the end of that time it was sold at a good price for tennis.

The next idea Mr Cochran hit upon was to run the Olympia Annexe as a Midget City, and he collected no fewer than a hundred dwarfs, including Countess Magri, who was formerly Mrs General Tom Thumb. He began by giving forty of the little folk dinner at the Savoy at a huge circular table in the middle of the public restaurant. Next day the whole town was talking of the party.

Countess Magri was an American and had four brothers and sisters all nearly six feet high. But she was tiny. She was a very well-educated and highly intelligent woman. At one time she had retired into private life, but was so stared at that in the end she preferred to go back to the stage.

One of the dwarfs was a Hindu named Smaun Sing

Hpoo, who was a wonderful gymnast and whose act on the rings was as fine as any by a full-grown performer.

Boxing is a chancy business, so far as profits are concerned, but Mr Cochran was always ready to take chances. One of his first finds was Gus Ruhlin, whose fight with Sharkey was one of the most tremendous heavyweight contests ever seen. Sharkey took punishment beyond what any human being could have been expected to take and lasted eleven rounds.

Later Mr Cochran arranged the match between Billy Wells and Joe Beckett at the Holborn Stadium. He paid the fighters £600 each. But since the receipts were £3344 2*s*. 0*d*. the business panned out very well. Beckett knocked out Wells, but that was simply because Wells was so wretchedly nervous. Another big success was the fight between Wells and Colin Bell at Olympia. There was a very fine lightweight contest the same night between Summers and Stone, and Mr Cochran put up £2500 in purses for the two contests, yet made a handsome profit. But that, mind you, was in 1914, long before the days of million-dollar fights.

Things did not always work out so well. Mr Cochran arranged a fight between Wilde and Mansfield, paying Wilde £1000 and Mansfield £125. The gate receipts were only £1000. When Beckett fought Goddard Mr Cochran had to pay Beckett £2500 and Goddard £2000. The entire prize-money for that night was just about £5000, but in this case the gate realized £8000. Quite a nice profit! Goddard, an ex-Guardsman, was six feet three and a half, and weighed fourteen stone, a splendid specimen of a man. But Beckett knocked him out in the second round.

£8000 seems a lot of gate-money, but a little later,

when Mr Cochran organized an enormous triple bill at Olympia, the gate receipts were £18,860. When this triple bill was first advertised many people thought that the promoter had gone mad, and one paper actually had an interview with him as to his sanity. The climax came when Mr Cochran arranged the fight between Beckett and Carpentier. It had to take place at the Holborn Stadium, and people gasped when the prices of admission were advertised. Ring-side seats twenty-five guineas, standing-room at five guineas. The place was packed, and the receipts were close on £30,000, a record for England. The betting was all on Beckett, but Carpentier knocked him out within seventy-three seconds.

The day after this fight Carpentier's manager signed a new contract in Mr Cochran's office for a fight between Carpentier and Dempsey—Carpentier to receive £20,000 win, lose, or draw. Almost at once some French promoters came along with a bigger offer, and then the news arrived that Mr William Fox of Fox Films was in the ring with an offer of over half a million dollars. Mr Cochran himself went to New York to arrange matters, and stayed at the Knickerbocker Hotel. His reputation had gone before him, and his telephone never stopped ringing. He had offers of oil-fields, motor factories, farms, everything down to a baker's shop. After a while the other promoters fell out, and it came to a battle between the well-known Tex Rickard and Mr Cochran.

In the end the two came to an agreement, and Mr Cochran hurried back to London, but on the way home became desperately ill, and was told he must give up all thoughts of business for a long time to come. He was put to bed, and remained there for two months. As he says himself, the illness could not have come at a worse time. He was forced to throw everything overboard, and lost a fortune. But in all the really big boxing-matches he had organized not one was a failure from a financial point of view.

After a long holiday in Spain Mr Cochran came back to London, where he had arranged to reopen the old Oxford Music-hall with his *League of Notions.* He had meant to spend £25,000 on transforming this old theatre, but the alterations actually cost nearer £80,000, and then the opening was delayed for over a month owing to his illness. In rent and salaries the delay meant a loss of £400 a day, which will give the reader some idea of the risks a showman has to run.

The expenses were enormous. He had brought silks from America, Batik work from New York, and had silks specially made at Lyons. The new show went amazingly, and for some time played to £4000 a week, that is £1500 profit. Then came strikes, and business went down. At the end of ten months' run the profit was only £7000, instead of £20,000 as it should have been.

Another disastrous show for Mr Cochran was *Mayfair and Montmartre.* There was nothing wrong with the revue itself, and for the first six weeks it showed a profit of £1200 a week. Then Delysia's throat got bad, and her doctor forbade her to use her voice. The whole revue had been built round Delysia, and her loss killed it. Mr Cochran lost £20,000.

These cases are quoted just to show the risks of a showman's career. Illness is one of those things that it is impossible for him to guard against. Another is weather. In 1923 Mr Cochran had six plays running in London besides a Sacha Guitry season at the New Oxford, and his expenses were £17,500 a week. All went well until a hot spell, and when this came a big profit dropped to a loss of £2000 a week.

On the other hand, when Mr Cochran had *Dover Street to Dixie* running at the Pavilion not even hot weather could kill the interest of the public in that wonderful coloured actress Florence Mills, and receipts ran as high as £3000 a week.

The Rodeo or Cowboy Championship at the Wembley Stadium was another of Mr Cochran's ideas. It started splendidly, yet at the end there was no profit. The venture came out square, without profit or loss, but it had meant six months' hard work for nothing.

It is safe to say that there is no other character of those whose stories are told in this book who has had a more varied or interesting life than Mr Charles Cochran, none who has met more interesting people, no one else who has made or lost larger sums of money, perhaps none who has more friends. And if he lost money he never lost his honour or his pluck.

SIR ARTHUR DUCKHAM
Photo Mesdames Morter

CHAPTER IV

TURNING £250 INTO A FORTUNE

The Story of Sir Arthur Duckham

IF any trade expert were asked what has been the aim of British industries during the past thirty years the answer would be, "To search for improved methods of doing everyday jobs." Science, chemistry, research—in other words, the skilled knowledge of trained minds—have been playing a steadily increasing part in industry, until to-day the expert often receives a larger salary than the business man for whom he works.

It is sometimes said that no boy has any chance of becoming an expert unless his parents are rich enough to pay for a long and costly training. That is not true. It is hard work rather than money which is necessary in order to enter the ranks of those who are the inventors of to-day. Even in the coal industry, in connexion with which more is spent upon research than for any other British industry, at least two of the greatest experts living began life as poor boys, faced with all the difficulties that probably troubled many of our readers. This chapter is about one of those men, who, without money or influence, has risen from the bottom rung of the ladder to the top.

Arthur McDougal Duckham was born at Blackheath and educated at Blackheath School. Schooldays over at seventeen, he decided to become an engineer, and served his apprenticeship like any other boy. There are all sorts of engineers. Duckham saw that it was advisable to specialize in one job, and so he devoted his time to furnace-work and coal-carbonization—the branch of engineering which has brought to our homes the gas which cooks our foods, heats our rooms, and in many cases lights them as well.

The technical development of the gas industry was then still in its infancy, and the wages that could be earned by a young man without special qualifications small. But Arthur Duckham was content to wait, and meanwhile to learn all he could. While in the workshop he spent his evenings at King's College, London, studying technical engineering. And when he got back to his bedroom late at night he would sit and plan the developments which his quick brain already saw might be carried out to make the gas industry more efficient.

At nineteen years of age, when earning thirty shillings a week, he took a step which seemed likely to jeopardize all his dreams of bold bids for fame. He got engaged. The wise ones shook their heads. He was too young. And he had no money. His prospects, they said, would be ruined if he saddled himself with the responsibilities of a wife and home. First make your fortune and then find your wife, he was told.

Duckham's answer was to secure a post as assistant engineer to the Bournemouth Gas and Water Company at a starting salary of £4 a week. In those days that was something very near real wealth, and when shortly afterward this was raised to £5 a week he took the plunge and got married.

With a wife to support he was more determined to

progress than ever. And fortunately his chief at Bournemouth, Colonel Woodall, was just as anxious to improve the methods of manufacturing gas as was the young 'second in command.' Together they began to study the question of inventing a method for the continuous carbonization of coal. The process is complicated and need not be explained here, although it is one of the wonders of modern industry which every boy will find fascinating to study.

These two men, developing their own ideas in their spare time after hard working-days, produced a new method of making gas which has since revolutionized the industry, and is to-day used in half the gasworks in this country.

Having patented their invention, the next step was to convince gas companies that it would work. To do that some one had to leave a safe job and run the risk of making no money at all in the event of failure. The man who took that risk was Arthur Duckham. He threw up his safe job as assistant engineer, and with a capital of £250 which he had borrowed he set out to convince the gas industry that his invention was of value and would save them money.

He met with more sympathy than he had expected, but still success was not easy. He had many moments when hope was all but dead. For nearly six years he worked harder than ever before on the patent which was all that stood between himself and failure. During those vital years he sometimes worked for two days and two nights without stopping, and frequently he worked the clock round. His normal day lasted for 14 hours, for he realized that if success was to be won it could only be by his own efforts.

Like all new things the retort which constituted his invention did not always work well after it had been constructed. In these cases Duckham's simple plan was to keep on working at it until satisfactory results were obtained.

In one case the young engineer secured a contract, although his estimate was not the lowest of those submitted. He asked the engineer to the company why they had given him the job.

" I've been watching the work of all you fellows throughout the country," said the engineer. " You have all been making every silly mistake that could be made, but you have profited by your mistakes. The others haven't."

During these years, while he was slowly building up what are now known as the " Woodall-Duckham Companies " and getting works to take up the retort which they had invented, Arthur Duckham found that a happy marriage was his greatest aid to success. Never for an instant, even when things looked blackest, did either his wife or he regret the " rash step " of marrying on £5 a week. That marriage had made a man of him—had made it necessary for him to delete the word ' failure ' from his vocabulary altogether. He was too busy building success to contemplate the opposite.

The work which he had chosen was no bed of roses, apart altogether from the long hours. We can imagine that many boys would have regarded it as too hard to be endured. It meant working for long hours close—sometimes too close—to hot furnaces, where there was always the danger of getting badly burnt.

Often Duckham worked on one of his plants in a temperature so excessive that one man would be playing a hose on him all the time to prevent his clothing from catching alight. To this day he bears on his chest the marks of a burn eighteen inches long, which he got by leaning against a piece of hot iron. It was killing work, but it was all part of the career he had chosen, and he liked it.

When there was a particularly hot job to be done Duckham and his fellow-workers would toss up to see who should undertake it. One day they spun a coin to see who should go down into a hot retort and fetch up a steel plate. Duckham won, and the other man went down, his hand and arm swathed in asbestos, which enabled him to hold the great tongs used for moving hot steel without getting burnt. Duckham stood by playing a hose on the man's arms and clothes to prevent him from getting burnt, and was so keen on keeping the fellow cool that he forgot how near he stood to the heat, and only remembered when his own trousers were alight and his legs badly burnt.

That is an example of the risks of the job. And there were disappointments too. Such as the day when he was to show one of his new plants to a gathering of engineers at Liverpool. He travelled up to Lancashire overnight and worked for twenty hours in getting everything ready. The following day he delivered a lecture to the experts, and then proceeded to lead them to the plant upon which he had laboured so long and lovingly—only to find that while he had been talking a fog had rolled up, and no one could see anything at all.

That sort of set-back only made him all the keener to make his ideas known. He forgot all about the clock, and slept only that he might arise refreshed for further work—the work which he never doubted would one day mean success.

Despite the strain and hard work of that time, however, he always found time for plenty of exercise. The successful man in the battle of life is the fit man, and Arthur Duckham had learnt that no man can stand the strain of hard work who neglects to keep body and muscles in condition.

In six years the battle had been won. More inventions were perfected, and the name Duckham began to stand for success in gasworks construction. It might have stood for success in something more romantic—Arthur Duckham might have built aeroplanes, or giant buildings, or warships, instead of gasworks. But the reader who sees romance only in picturesque things is making a big mistake. In improving the methods of producing gas Arthur Duckham was doing something which helped to make the homes of all of us more comfortable. Better gas and cheaper gas meant less smoke over our cities and more sunshine, less work for the housewife, more work for the miner as more and more coal was needed for the growing gas industry. Surely that was something worth doing ?

Here, in case you have not heard it, let us tell the famous story about the three men who were employed in breaking up stones which were destined to make the foundations of a new cathedral. A stranger, watching them at work, asked one man what he was doing.

" I'm breaking stones," he replied.

The stranger asked the second man.

" Earning a shilling an hour," was the answer.

Then the stranger noticed that the third man was

working harder than either of the others, and he approached him.

"You are working very hard," he said. "What are you doing?"

"I'm building a cathedral," answered the third man—the man with vision.

When Arthur Duckham set out to invent a vertical retort he wasn't just finding a way of making money. Nor was he just tinkering about with so much steel and so many plans. He was helping to make the gas industry, one of the most important in this country, bigger and more efficient. And he did it.

The Woodall-Duckham Company started with the tiny capital of £100. To-day its turnover is £1,000,000 a year, and its founder has become Sir Arthur Duckham, K.C.B., M.Inst.C.E., a member of the Sankey Coal Commission, a former Director-General of aircraft production, and the first President of the Institute of Chemical Engineers. Not a bad record for a boy who started on 30*s.* a week? And a few months ago, at the invitation of the British Government, Sir Arthur Duckham went to Australia as the head of a special trade delegation, sent out to assist the development of trade between the Commonwealth and the Motherland.

He left behind a son, Richard Duckham, whose training has been planned in the light of the lessons which his father learned during his years of hard work. At twelve years of age Sir Arthur Duckham's son is a useful bricklayer, carpenter, and mechanic. He can already take down a small car completely, overhaul it, and put it together again. He has done it as well as any garage could have done the job. The boy has many friends, among them engineers and other artisans, and he never loses an opportunity of learning how to do anything connected with machinery. And his father believes in allowing him to think for himself, without worrying about conventional things. According to Sir Arthur Duckham, it is just as important for a boy to be able to use his hands as his head, and he sees that whatever work interests young Richard is properly learned and performed.

Sir Arthur Duckham himself has progressed from the bottom of the ladder to the top in thirty years. And at the end of that time, anxious to help other boys to follow in his footsteps, he looks back over his life and declares that " the secret of success lies in giving a little over-measure on every job undertaken—to do a little more than is expected of you every time."

CHAPTER V

THE MAN WHO INVENTED A HOBBY

George Eastman, the Kodak King

JUST over fifty years ago a young American bank-clerk at Rochester, New York State, was hauled up before the manager and reprimanded for always turning up at the bank with stained fingers and thumbs.

" I can't help it," he replied. " The chemicals which I use for my photographic experiments leave their mark behind, however careful I am."

The manager was sympathetic, but business was business—and the upshot of the interview was that the young man was told that he must either give up photography or give up the bank.

He thought it over, took his courage in both hands, and gave up the bank, preferring to face the possibility of poverty rather than give up his beloved photography.

Half a century later—in 1926—that young bank-clerk, now a millionaire and the head of a vast business whose trade-mark is known in every country in the world, made a gift of £200,000 to a London hospital to set up a dental clinic, and at about the same time he celebrated his own seventy-second birthday by sailing for East Africa on a big-game hunting expedition.

Between those two dates the young clerk, named

George Eastman, had crowded a career as dramatic as any on record.

The beginning of that career was a desire to make money.

George Eastman was a practically-minded boy, without many of the dreams which have kept alive the flagging hopes of other great inventors when success would not come. His father had died young after founding one of the first business colleges in the United States. This school provided the widow and son with the means to live for some years, but eventually it failed, and George Eastman, then fourteen years of age, was faced with the urgent necessity to find work so that he could support his mother.

After one or two small jobs he secured a junior post in the Rochester branch of a bank, where he had ample opportunity of studying the customers and trying to detect why some of them always had plenty of money in their accounts and others hardly ever had any. Money and the need for it interested Eastman more than anything else in those days, and it was not long before he realized that if he wanted anything more than a modest steady salary he would have to get out of the bank and find some other means of keeping the home going.

So he started keeping his eyes open for a means of starting business on his own. He had already realized, as Henry Ford did when a young man, that to win real success he must become the proprietor of some article of universal appeal—something that every one would want.

Henry Ford, as you will read in this volume, thought either watches or motor-cars the most promising things to sell, and chose motors. George Eastman could not for a long time decide what sort of invention offered any hope of success—or even whether he was clever enough to invent anything at all. If the reader will sit down now and try to think of some idea which he could make and sell at a profit, it will be realized how hard a task the young bank-clerk set himself.

George Eastman might have been searching for some idea worth money to this day but for a summer holiday which the bank gave him at a time when his mother was not well enough to go away with him.

He had planned to go to the West Indies, a trip which seemed like real adventure to a young man who had rarely been out of his own town, and as his mother could not go he decided to learn the new method of picture-making, or photography, before he went and purchase a camera, so that he could take some photographs of the scenes he visited and bring them back for his mother.

Learning photography in those days was a very different thing from taking snapshots to-day. His first lesson from the local photographer taught him how to pack upon his back the apparatus necessary to take the simplest picture; this included a large box-camera, a heavy tripod, glass plates, nitrate bath, water-carrier, and dark tent. Before a single photograph could be taken all this equipment had to be carried to the spot selected, and set up—a work taking an hour. In the dark tent the photographer had to mix solutions to sensitize the glass plates, slip them into the camera dripping wet, take the photograph, and then dive back into the darkness of the tent and develop the plates on the spot.

To take a single photograph under these conditions was a hard afternoon's work, and photography, instead of being a pleasure, was real labour. His experiences o that holiday, plodding along hot roads, loaded like a mule with his photographic materials, convinced George Eastman that taking pictures ought to be made easier for the holiday-maker.

He pondered over the idea for some time before he realized that here, perhaps, was the chance of making money for which he had been searching. "Why shouldn't I find a new method of taking pictures which does away with half the work ?" he asked his mother, and straightway he began his experiments.

Enthusiasm means far more to the inventor than expensive equipment. The romance of George Eastman's story lies not so much in what he did as in the fact that when he began experimenting he had nowhere to work except the kitchen sink and his mother's stove.

Later he managed to get a room for his own use, and there he used to work after leaving the bank until midnight or after, convinced that any day he would make the discovery he was after—a photographic plate which could be dried and sold in packets, doing away with the necessity for sensitizing it and developing it as soon as the photograph had been taken.

He got one hint from an English magazine; all other ideas he read were tried out. Every day his hobby became more and more the real business of his life. And at last, after two years' hard work, he invented the dry plate.

His first 'factory' consisted of one room over a shop. Here he began to manufacture his plates with the help of one assistant. After leaving the bank at night he went to his room and mixed the emulsion, which was applied to the plates the next day by his assistant.

It made a mess of his hands, but sales were growing, and when the lady clerk working next to him in the bank complained to the manager George Eastman had sufficient confidence in his invention to resign his job rather than shut down his tiny business.

Soon after this a New York photographic dealer on holiday met a Rochester man taking photographs with Eastman's dry plates, which were still unknown outside the Rochester district. The New York man realized what the invention meant and got George Eastman's address. The next day he called at the tiny Eastman factory and gave an order for a definite number of plates monthly, to be paid for upon delivery. This was just what George Eastman wanted to enable him to increase his output, and he booked the order joyfully.

For some months all was well. When winter came and the New York dealer continued to take the same number of plates each month, although very few photographs were taken in the winter, George Eastman decided that he would soon be able to extend his factory.

Then came spring, and the blow fell. Customers who bought the plates which had been on the dealer's shelves all the winter reported that they would not take good photographs. The dealer used some of the plates himself, and found them all foggy. So he came to Eastman to know the cause of it. That was the first that the young inventor knew about his plates being perishable. But it was so—the gelatine aged and would not keep more than a certain time.

It was a big blow, and it meant facing a bigger one. For the question arose of who should stand the loss of that big stock of useless plates which the dealer had collected on his shelves. They had all been bought and paid for in good faith. Neither Eastman nor the dealer knew they would 'go bad.' Yet they were useless.

Some young men might have tried to invent excuses for not returning the money. George Eastman already thought of himself as a great manufacturer, and he knew that the most valuable asset a manufacturer can have is a name for straight dealing. There and then he took back every plate and refunded the whole of the money. It cleaned him out, so that he had hardly a pound left, but he was prepared to stand the loss rather than make an unworthy excuse.

He had taken a partner into his business now to provide the extra capital needed, and together they set about the task of restoring their vanished profits, taking care, however, to warn all purchasers that the plates would not keep beyond a certain time. Business boomed. George Eastman's dry plate was being discussed and written about in all parts of America. It looked as though the bank-clerk had carved success for himself out of one idea before reaching the age of thirty. Then came the greatest crisis of his life. One day he was thinking happily of bigger success, of capturing new markets—the next he found himself facing complete and utter ruin.

George Eastman was little more than a boy when it happened, and few boys can have faced such a complete catastrophe with greater courage. Eastman's emulsion—the invention which had made the dry plate possible—suddenly refused to work. His plates became useless. And what was worse, the most careful investigations failed to discover any reason for this failure.

Night and day he went over his formula, checking every detail. He made emulsion in the way he had always made it, using exactly the same chemicals and methods. Everything was the same except the plates; and they would not take photographs. As though struck down, his business simply disappeared. Until he could discover what had happened he could not make another plate, or another penny. Disaster faced him and his band of helpers. They closed down the factory, while day and night Eastman worked there in his laboratory, getting more and more frantic as experiment after experiment failed. It was as though he had been dreaming, as though dry plates had never been made by his formula at all. If they had, why did the same methods and chemicals fail to make them now?

Then one day George Eastman disappeared. He was not seen at his factory again for a month. In that time he dashed across to England, and from the best firm of plate-makers abroad he had bought a formula which would save him. The day after he returned his factory was once more working overtime, turning out plates for the new season's trade. He was saved. But how narrow a squeak it had been, and what that crisis meant to Eastman, may be judged from the fact that during those four weeks that he was away from Rochester his hair had turned grey before the age of thirty!

And now comes the strangest part of the story. Eastman eventually found that the reason for the failure of his own formula was that a particular delivery of gelatine which he had used for the first was exhausted, and he had bought a second supply which did not give the same results. Further experiments showed that it was some impurity in the first consignment of gelatine which had given the good results in the case of his first plates. This impurity was absent from the new stock, and so, although the plates were made in exactly the same way, they were unsatisfactory. And more remarkable still, no other batch of the same material gave him good results from that day to this. In other words, Eastman's discovery was due to some imperfection in his gelatine which he did not know existed and which he has never been able to repeat. But the original stock lasted long enough to make his astounding career possible.

Having surmounted this crisis with the aid of the formula purchased in England, he set about the task of making photography even easier. He found it in a 'film' made of paper, which could be treated in the emulsion and weighed less than the heavy glass plates then in use.

It was the new film, made in a roll and loaded into a hand camera, which brought photography within the reach of the amateur for the first time. It caught on, and, seeing the chance of selling this new picture-making method in foreign countries, Eastman searched for a trademark which could be pronounced in any language. The result of his search was a new word which has since made his films famous throughout the world—the word Kodak.

His film was still being developed toward the celluloid film which every boy knows to-day, when Eastman was approached by Edison who wanted to know whether it was true that Eastman had invented a transparent film. Learning that it was so, Edison asked to be allowed to buy some for use in a machine he had just invented called the kinetoscope, which projected pictures to the eye of a peep-hole and which, given a transparent picture, would throw it from the film on to a screen some distance away.

The film was supplied to him, and for five years both men experimented upon their connected problems. In that time Edison perfected the first film-projector, and Eastman produced a celluloid film which would pass light through itself, and solved at one stroke both his own problem of popular photography and Edison's problem of the moving picture.

Thus it was these two men—Edison with his kinetoscope and Eastman with his transparent film—who made the whole vast moving picture industry possible.

Even with the coming of the transparent film Eastman did not rest. Other improvements occupied his time while his business continued to expand. The folding camera came next, then the developing tank that was smaller than the old-time cameras had been. Lenses were improved, and step by step the pocket camera as we know it to-day was brought into being.

George Eastman had set out to make money, and he had made it. He made so much of it that long ago he ceased to think about money, and went on because he wanted to see all the world taking those 'happy snaps' of their holidays without carting about all the heavy apparatus which was necessary when he went to the West Indies as a boy.

In bringing the camera within the reach of every one his business has grown until to-day it encircles the earth. The largest Kodak factory, in the United States, covers a square mile of ground and comprises 120 buildings of from seven to fourteen stories high. In that giant factory there is a staff of 20,000 people performing over 250 different jobs. Thus one building takes rags and makes them into photographic paper, another makes the boxes in which Kodaks and films are exported.

Silver bromide or silver chloride is used to make the films sensitive to light, and this one factory uses more silver in the course of a year than any other place, except the Mint.

No less than two hundred thousand miles of cinema film is made by the Kodak company every year. During the summer of 1928 George Eastman announced yet another new invention—films which will make moving pictures in colour. One side of the new film is covered with minute corrugations, and part of these catch each of the primary colours, both when scenes are photographed and when they are projected through a colour screen. This latest invention of the ' camera wizard ' will enable amateur motion picture photographers, whose cameras may now be equipped at a cost of a few pounds, to take colour films.

And all this vast industry, as large to-day in Britain as in the United States, is due to a young bank-clerk's working in a tiny one-room factory with one assistant. George Eastman has proved that there is no limit to the success which can be gained with the aid of the right idea—plus hard work and enthusiasm.

CHAPTER VI

THE WORLD'S FIRST BILLIONAIRE!

How Henry Ford Built 15,000,000 Cars

ON July 30, 1863, there was born on a farm at Dearborn, Michigan, a boy who was destined to accomplish several surprising things which had never been achieved before.

His parents were fairly prosperous farmers—though poor, for most American farmers had a struggle to make both ends meet in those days—and when the neighbours asked Mr Ford, the boy's father, what he intended to do with Henry when he grew up the father replied, " Oh, he'll take on the farm later on."

That farmhouse is still standing, and Henry Ford has " taken it on," but not in the way his father intended. For the farmer's boy invented a motor-car which made his name famous, built and sold fifteen millions of them, and became the world's first billionaire. And in making himself the most successful business man of this or any other generation he transformed the village in which he had been born into the thriving, bustling centre of the Ford Motor Works—and bought up the farm, along with most of the other parts of the place.

We wonder how many of the millions of boys who have laughed over the first Ford joke—the one about giving a squirrel with every car to run behind and pick up the nuts—realizes that it was this farmer's boy and his

'Tin Lizzie' which brought the motor-car within the reach of millions who, up to the coming of the Ford, had regarded it as a luxury for the very rich?

In the United States, where motors are called automobiles, they have a saying that Henry Ford was the man who put the 'mob' in automobiles. But Henry Ford's career is anything but a joke. This remarkable man had to face terrible discouragement and difficulties in his early days, had to surmount at least one great financial crisis after he had become famous. Like every successful man he had faith in himself and faith in his own brain. And he has been justified. For some years his income has been in the neighbourhood of £400,000 a week, and the wages bill at the Ford Works is something like £200,000,000 a year. All made possible by perseverance, for if Ford had listened to those who regarded his dream of a cheap motor-car as 'cranky' he would still have been either a poor farmer or at best a jobbing engineer repairing farming machinery.

Henry Ford's first idea about life was that there was too much work done by hand on the farm. He was a born engineer, and he dreamt about machinery being used to do the heavy jobs, so that ten times as much work could be got through in a day by the same number of people. Those were the days before any farm machinery had been invented, however, and so Ford's dreams remained just dreams.

But as he grew to manhood he became more and more certain that what the world was waiting for was the coming of the popular machine, a car which would carry people about and make their work easier.

By the time he was twelve he had collected a pocketful of trinkets—bolts and nuts picked up in odd places.

They were useless, of course, but he felt sure that when he was older they would come in useful.

That year there happened the first two great events of his life. He saw for the first time a vehicle not pulled by horses—a crude road steam-wagon, operated by a boiler stoked with coal like a locomotive. The sight of that engine, primitive as it was, centred all his thoughts upon making a better road engine which every one could buy. He knew it was the first step along the pathway of his thoughts, and so he began to turn over in his mind how such a machine could be built. Some years later he actually constructed a road steam-engine similar to the one he had seen—not because he imagined it was the best that could be made for its purpose, but just to prove to his own satisfaction that he could build one.

The other big event of his twelfth year was being given his first watch.

That watch was a machine which he could experiment with. By studying it he learnt more about the construction of watches than is known by most jewellers. He took it to pieces and put it together again. It went. Bolder after this success, he offered to try to repair broken watches for his friends. At the age of fifteen he was an experienced watch-repairer, although from first to last he only possessed amateur tools which he had fashioned for himself.

His parents frowned upon this interest in machinery, and when Henry left school at the age of seventeen there were many discussions at the Ford home before he got his way and was allowed to apprentice himself to a local engineering works.

Long before his three years' apprenticeship was over Henry Ford had qualified as a machinist. But even this progress was not sufficiently rapid to satisfy him, and so he worked in the evenings repairing watches for a local jeweller.

His expert knowledge of watches caused him to consider the idea of building a watch, manufactured entirely by machinery, which could be sold at 1*s.* 3*d.* But after prolonged thought, during which Henry Ford became the owner of over three hundred different watches, he decided to leave watches alone and stick to his original idea of one day making a road vehicle which would be both cheap and reliable.

It is interesting to consider to-day what the world would have lost had that young engineer produced a Ford watch instead of the Ford car. And here, in passing, it may be said that the success of another American, Samuel Ingersoll, the largest watch-manufacturer in the world, proves that Ford's idea of a cheap universal watch was not so foolish after all.

When his apprenticeship was completed Ford succeeded in getting a job with the local representative of the Westinghouse Company, who were selling a road engine very similar to the one which he had first seen on the road a few years before.

Ford was now an expert in the repair of these cumbersome road steam-engines, and when not working for the local company he settled down to build a steam-engine of his own. The story of that engine is told in his own words in his book, *My Life and Work* (Heinemann).

> It had a kerosene-heated boiler, and it developed plenty of power and a neat control—which is so easy with a steam throttle. But the boiler was dangerous. To get the requisite power without too big and heavy a power-plant required that

the engine work under high pressure ; sitting on a high-pressure steam-boiler is not altogether pleasant. To make it even reasonably safe required an excess of weight that nullified the economy of the high pressure. For two years I kept experimenting with various sorts of boilers—the engine and control problems were simple enough—and then I definitely abandoned the whole idea of running a road vehicle by steam. I knew that in England they had what amounted to locomotives running on the roads hauling lines of trailers, and also there was no difficulty in designing a big steam-tractor for use on a large farm. But ours were not then English roads; they would have stalled or racked to pieces the strongest and heaviest road-tractor. And, anyway, the manufacturing of a big tractor which only a few wealthy farmers could buy did not seem to me worth while.

Ford now began to look round for some other method of making a light road vehicle, and he found it in the Otto internal-combustion engine then being tried out in England. By a fortunate chance an Otto engine, fed with vaporized petrol, had been imported into the district and needed repairing. Ford was by now supposed to know more about engines than any other man in the district, so the job of repairing it came to him.

This piece of luck enabled him to study a petrol engine at first hand, and in 1885 he built an engine worked on the same principles. It was successful, but most people who had ever heard of their existence still regarded these petrol engines as 'toys,' and Ford's first attempt aroused no enthusiasm.

About this time Henry Ford returned to the farm. His father still considered that his son was wasting his time, and Ford himself wanted more time for his experiments. He also wanted to get married. So when his father offered him forty acres of timber, providing Ford would give up ideas of being a mechanic, Henry Ford agreed to return to the farm for a time, got married, and fitted himself up with a sawmill and a portable engine to cut his timber into commercial lengths.

In a little house thirty-one feet square Henry Ford and his wife began their married life. The outlook wasn't bright, but Ford still believed that the chance to make a road vehicle which every one would want was coming. So after working on the timber all day he read every book on engines he could find.

He had begun work on a new and improved petrol engine on the farm, when he got the chance of an engineer's job with the Detroit Electric Company. He took it and moved with his wife into that city. And so it came about that the townspeople of Detroit were privileged, in 1893, to see Henry Ford driving his first motor-car along the roadway.

At the time most people did not regard the queer contraption which Henry Ford had at last made to go as any asset to the town. This first motor-car which Detroit had ever seen was, in fact, an unmitigated nuisance. It frightened horses, blocked the traffic. Henry Ford relates that if he left it for a minute in the street, some one would always try to start it 'for a joke.' With the result that he had to carry a chain and padlock it to a lamp-post when he went into a shop.

The police disliked the first Ford car as much as the townspeople did. They badgered Ford for exceeding the speed limit, and made him get a special permit to run it from the mayor of the town. Thus Ford held the first motor-licence issued in the United States.

Ford No. 1—the forerunner of over fifteen million Fords—carried Henry Ford and his friends for over a

HENRY FORD IN THE FIRST FORD CAR 70

Photo Topical

thousand miles in two years. Then he sold it for two hundred dollars, or £40 in English money, and used the money to build a better one.

The second car was lighter than the first and possessed gears. Soon after it was built Henry Ford reached the turning-point of his life. The Edison Company offered him the post of superintendent of their works, providing he would give up his 'time-wasting' experiments on motor-cars.

As Ford himself puts it, "I had to choose between my job and my motor-car. I chose the motor-car, or rather I gave up my job—there was really nothing in the way of choice. For already I knew that the car was bound to be a success. I quit my job on August 15, 1899, and went into the motor business."

It was a huge risk which he took. His income was only just enough to enable them to live and leave over a few pounds for further experiments. If a successful car could not be made Ford was doomed to failure. But he took the risk smiling, and so did Mrs Ford, who knew her man better than anyone else. Never for an instant did she doubt his ultimate success.

A group of business men put up the money to found a motor-company, and Ford became their chief engineer. They were business men, and in the new business for profits. So their idea was to build a few cars and make a big profit on each one. Ford's idea, since he had been a boy of twelve, was to build cars by the thousand and make a small profit on each one. But he only held a tiny portion of the capital, and for the next few years had to do as he was told.

In March 1902 Henry Ford resigned his position with the company. He had resolved to work on his own, and never again did he take a position in which he was under the orders of others.

Those were the days when motor-racing was all the rage. The public had not grasped the fact that the new engines would transform their daily lives, and were only interested in motors when they ran against each other at speed trials.

Ford was not interested in speed. What he wanted to do was to make life more comfortable for every one, but particularly for the countryman, by building a car which the ordinary man could drive and could afford to buy. But the only way to get the public interested in motors was to enter the speed contest which other manufacturers had started, so Ford's first job after starting on his own was to rent a brick shed in Detroit, and there build two cars which could hold their own with the fastest then known.

One of these two cars won a big race, with the next competitor half a mile behind at the finish. Henry Ford did not drive the car, but he had tested it previously, and he afterward declared that driving that car was like "going over Niagara Falls."

He had proved that he could build a fast car. And after building about twenty-five various cars from the day when he drove his first crazy vehicle along the streets of Detroit he believed that the time had come to start manufacturing in earnest. So in 1903 Henry Ford took the plunge and formed the Ford Motor Company.

He was determined that this time there should be no one in a position to give him orders. Henry Ford was vice-president, designer, master mechanic, and general manager of the new company, and he held a quarter of the capital. The total funds of the company were less than £6000. That £6000 was the only money ever received by the company apart from profits put back into the business. And out of that acorn grew the millions which made Henry Ford the world's first billionaire.

In 1906 Henry Ford decided to increase his holding in the company to 51 per cent, so that he would have absolute control. And after three years' working he was already rich enough to pay the sum required out of his savings. Thirteen years later, when Edsel Ford, his son, bought up the remaining shares, the price paid was £2500 for each £20 share, and the total amount required to buy less than half of that original £6000 invested was fifteen millions!

The Ford Motor Company began in a carpenter's shop. All the parts of the first cars were manufactured elsewhere. Henry Ford designed the car, and assembled the parts when they were received from the factories.

In the first year he made and sold 1708 cars, an enormous advance on any previous output. These were the Model "A" cars—the first real Fords. In the second year Ford accepted the advice of his partners and tried out two other models, with the result that output did not increase, and they sold only 1695 cars.

The first signs of the Ford 'boom' which carried the name of the farmer's son all over the world did not come until Henry Ford had secured absolute control of the company in 1906. Then he instituted the policy of one car at the cheapest price.

Events proved that Ford was right, and those who wanted to manufacture four or five different models were wrong.

The price of the 'popular' Ford car was cut to £120—

an unheard-of figure in those days—and within a year sales had jumped to 8423 cars.

Mass production now began in earnest. In one week during May 1908 the Ford works assembled 311 cars in six working days. In one day during June 1908 exactly one hundred cars were turned out. The Ford boom had begun—the little country boy who repaired watches in the evenings was already ahead of all his competitors.

The cars sold up to 1908 were the same as the Ford cars which every boy remembers, but much heavier. Henry Ford spent years searching for a material which would give strength without undue weight. At last he found it, and at the beginning of the 1908 winter season he placed on the market the first Model "T" Ford car, weighing only 1200 pounds.

The company had now been working for five years. In that time it had increased its works from a carpenter's shop to a factory covering two and a half acres. The number of workers employed had risen from 300 to 2000. And the profits had risen in proportion.

Model "T" was placed on the market, and its instant success showed Ford that here was the car he had been waiting for. In the first year he sold 10,607 'Tin Lizzies,' and from that moment he went right ahead, turning out this amazing car, until by 1925 no fewer than fifteen millions had been sold in all parts of the world.

At the end of 1908 Ford announced that in future the Ford Motor Company was going to build only one model—Model "T"—and that every car would have the same chassis. Furthermore, he remarked—and the remark has become famous—that "customers could have their cars painted any colour they liked, so long as it was black." In other words, the days of experiments were over, henceforth there would only be one Ford, and all Fords would be as alike as two peas.

His rivals, the men without the vision of Ford, declared that the company would be bankrupt within six months. What happened? By 1911 the factory space had grown from two and a half to thirty-two acres. The number of men employed had doubled, and the output of cars had risen from the 6000 odd of 1908 to 35,000 in 1911.

Meanwhile Henry Ford had introduced his car into Great Britain. Many of our readers will remember the part which the Ford played in the Great War, when they were used on every front. But before that a Ford car had been driven to the top of Ben Nevis, 4406 feet high, without breaking down.

That 'stunt' made England and Scotland wake up to the virtues of the Ford, and within a year 14,000 had been sold in this country. Later Ford opened a factory in Manchester, first as an assembling station, but where now the British Ford is manufactured.

All this time Henry Ford was devising methods of keeping pace with his increasing output. The greatest time-saving method of all those which originated in the Ford factories was the method, now adopted in most motor-works, of the 'moving assembly line.' By this method, instead of the motor being built in one place, with each workman coming to it in turn, the engine or chassis was placed on a moving platform—rows of them—and all the workman had to do was to stand still and add his portion as it passed him.

This 'assembly line' was adjusted in its movement so that each workman had just enough time to add his particular part to the engine or chassis without hurry, but without the waste of a single second before the next engine reached him.

The result of this new idea in mass production was astounding. Henry Ford relates how in 1913, before the moving platform had been tried, it required nine hours and forty-five minutes of working time to build one motor. Six months later, under the new system, the time required had been reduced to five hours and fifty-six minutes. In other words the same number of workers could turn out twice as many cars a day in the same time. No wonder the wages were raised in the Ford works without any increase in the cost of the car to the customer.

Labour-saving methods of this sort, which really meant using the workers' time in a scientific manner, instead of so arranging things that half of it was wasted, enabled Ford to announce, in 1914, that in future the lowest-paid worker in his factories would be paid at the rate of £1 a day for an eight-hour day and a forty-eight hour week—the highest wage scale ever paid out by a great company. Following that announcement the number of cars produced rose from 248,000 to 308,000 in one year, while the price was actually reduced to under £100. Think of it—a motor-car selling at less than £100, made by workmen in factories where the men who swept the floors received £6 a week!

That apparent miracle had been made possible by mass production, by not wasting a second or a single scrap of material.

The success of Henry Ford's amazing career lay in producing a cheap car for the first time, but for the real romance of that career we must look at the way in which this man worked day and night, long after he had become a millionaire, to discover ways in which he could turn out more and more cars. From those early days on the farm Henry Ford had never wanted money for himself—few great men ever do. What he had wanted was to see the vast world public learning the joys of motoring for the first time. And that meant new methods and cheap cars. Henry Ford saw his dreams come true, for he found the new methods which made the cheap car possible.

But there was still one more difficulty to be overcome before Ford's success was proved to be impregnable. In order to enable his son Edsel to buy up the balance of the shares in the company during 1919, as mentioned earlier in this chapter, Henry Ford had borrowed £14,000,000. In 1920 there remained £7,000,000 of these notes outstanding, and his rivals began to circulate a rumour that Henry Ford was trying to borrow money—in other words that the Ford works were in some sort of financial difficulty.

A rumour of that sort can do a lot of damage, for nobody wants to buy a car if the company that make it is likely to go out of business and spare parts are going to be difficult to obtain. Moreover, Ford's policy had always been not to borrow a single penny. He knew that if once the financiers got a finger in the pie they would ask for stiff terms of such a rich company, and try to get some sort of control over the business. So he set about the task of finding that balance of £7,000,000 without borrowing a cent.

It was the biggest crisis which Henry Ford ever faced. There was one way in which he could do it—the contracts with the motor-dealers provided for payment in cash for all cars as delivered. He had orders for thousands in hand—therefore what he had to do was to so speed up production that when the day came for paying the balance of the money he would have enough cash in the bank to meet the claim.

He set about the task. Every method of increasing the output without increasing the cost was put into operation. The office staff was cut down by one-half, and those displaced were offered jobs in the factories, turning out more cars. Even the number of telephones was cut down as an economy measure.

Cars began to pour out at a higher rate than ever, and the prospects of getting that £7,000,000 seemed good, when Ford discovered that the Detroit, Toledo, and Ironton Railway, which carried the cars to the dealers, was delaying delivery of the necessary raw materials and parts, and also delaying delivery of the cars to the dealers. Now Ford cars on railway sidings brought in no cheques—only when the cars were delivered did the dealer pay. Unless delivery could be speeded up all his efforts were doomed to failure.

Ford considered this problem, and then played his trump card. He bought up the railway and gave orders that every Ford car was to be rushed through. By speeding up delivery of material to the factories he found that the time between the purchase of the material and the delivery of the completed car could be cut down from twenty-two to fourteen days. That meant that he could run his factories on smaller stocks. Small stocks meant less money locked up in materials. Cutting down railway-delivery times by one-third released £4,000,000 worth of stock and meant that much more in the bank.

The sum which Henry Ford needed between January 1 and April 1, 1921, to repay the loan and for the payment of income-tax and bonus on wages was £12,000,000. On January 1 the company possessed £4,000,000 of that sum. Then the great speed-up began, and four months later the Ford Motor Company had over £17,000,000 in the bank, or £5,000,000 more than was needed to pay every penny owing. It was the master stroke which saved Ford from going into the market to borrow money. And he had averted that fate by buying a whole railway just when things looked blackest! That was real courage—the sort of courage which he had shown when he threw up his job to begin manufacturing for himself. A smaller man would have written a letter of complaint to the railway company and hoped for the best. Ford did not waste a precious minute in letter-writing—he bought the railway and made sure of his deliveries.

That success put Henry Ford on his feet for all time. No one will ever challenge him again. When the famous Model "T" was taken off the market two years ago fifteen million of these cars had been sold in eighteen years. Since 1922 the Ford works had been turning them out at the rate of two million cars a year. Nothing like this had ever been known before, and it is doubtful if these amazing figures will ever be touched again, unless the new Ford car introduced in 1928 beats even the record of the old.

By 1925 the Ford companies were paying out more than fifty million pounds a year in wages to their own men. Counting the men working on contracts placed by Ford the companies were paying no less than two hundred million pounds a year in wage costs.

And the Ford car is still a one-man business, built up by the farmer's boy with a cranky notion of making a motor-car which the working-man could afford to buy.

Other men you may read about in this volume have had more adventurous careers, have travelled to the ends of the earth to find fortune, but none of them has become as rich as Henry Ford. And no other career of our generation is such a romance. Think of it—Henry Ford nearly became a manufacturer of cheap watches! As a boy watches fascinated him, and he had three hundred of them in his workshop. Since then other men have given the world cheap watches, but who would have thought out the 'Tin Lizzie' but the man who believed in its coming before he left school?

For the Ford car is more than a joke—it was the first of the hundreds of different makes of family cars which have helped to make life more comfortable for millions. And the fact that fifteen million people bought it proves that its inventor is one of the greatest business men of this or any other age.

A. W. GAMAGE

CHAPTER VII

"GOOD GOODS AND SMALL PROFITS"

The Story of A. W. Gamage

THEY say the seventh son is the brilliant one of the family. Mr Albert Walter Gamage was not the seventh, but the *seventeenth* child of his parents, and the youngest of the whole flock. He must have been a boy of very exceptional character to have risen as he has, for his father was a farmer who farmed a small area of stubborn Herefordshire clay, and had a hard struggle to make ends meet.

The youngest Gamage had no advantage of any kind, no education except that afforded by a village school, and the village school of sixty years ago taught reading and writing, but precious little else. He lived plainly, he worked hard out of school as well as in, and, barring a strong desire to get on, he does not seem to have shown any special promise of the amazing success which he has since attained.

While he was still quite a youngster a friend of his father offered him work in his shop in the little Buckinghamshire town of Winslow, and he jumped at the chance. Winslow is less than forty miles from London, so it was as a visitor from Winslow that young Gamage had his first sight of the capital—a sleepy sort of place compared with modern London. Horse-buses with back-to-back seats along the top—knife-boards they called them—

hansoms, growlers, horse-drawn carts and drays; no bicycles, for the bicycle existed only as a bone shaker in those days; one small length of underground railway; no electric light, no incandescent gas, no wood pavement; really very little of anything that makes up modern London as we know it to-day. Yet enough to fire the blood of young Gamage, who at once made up his mind to get work in London, and who did at last succeed in obtaining a place behind the counter of a drapery shop.

In the chapter on Mr Selfridge something will be said of the hard lot of the draper's assistant in early days. The hours were fearfully long, the pay wretched, and the chances of promotion so small as to be hardly worth considering. The only prospect to which an assistant could look forward was that of becoming shop-walker.

That is, if he remained on as assistant, but it is not to be supposed that Gamage ever looked upon his job as anything but a stepping-stone to much greater things. He knew from the beginning that the only chance for real success was to start on his own. But to start on your own you must have capital, and this young man had not a penny beyond his meagre wages. He set to work to save, and week by week managed to add a little to his slender store. In the same drapery house in which he was employed was another young salesman, by name Frank Spain, and he and Gamage talked much together. Gamage infected Spain with his own intense eagerness and made him save too.

One day Gamage took a watch to be cleaned to a small watchmaker's shop in Holborn, and as he chatted to the watchmaker the latter happened to remark that a hosier's shop was needed in that street. A chance! Never did trout rise to fly more fiercely than young

Gamage to this bait, yet that is a bad simile, because in this case the fish meant to have the bait and not the hook. He went back to Spain, and the two talked the thing over and decided to plunge. The next thing was to find a shop. Gamage found it, but the rent demanded was £220 a year, with a premium of £80 down for the lease. And he and Spain between them had just £150. No wonder that the two spent sleepless nights considering the risk and wondering if it were possible to undertake so much with so little behind them.

But when Gamage had once made up his mind his resolution was like iron. He took the shop, paying down £50 out of the £80 premium. Eight pounds was required for fittings, which left the new firm with less than £100 for stocking the shop. Gamage went to the wholesalers and asked for supplies on credit, which is quite the usual and orthodox way of starting, and then the first blow fell, for the wholesaler laughed at him, and refused to give a pennyworth of credit. "You have no capital," he said. "You will lose what little you have got. My advice is that you go back to your old place which is still open to you and give up this wild-cat idea."

It would be interesting to know what arguments Gamage used to convince that wholesaler, but probably it was personality rather than mere words which did the trick. At any rate the man of business changed his mind, and in the end decided to let this bold young fellow have all he asked for. And so the new little shop opened its doors, and you can imagine the hopes and fears of the two plucky young partners.

This was in 1878, and the small volume which was both cash-book and ledger in that year is still among the treasures of the head of the great firm in Holborn. It shows that the first week's trade amounted to £24. The second was not quite so good, for it was only £21, but the third showed a fine jump to £40. Then there was a drop to £36, caused by a day of very bad weather. It snowed all day, and no customers came in until the evening. The total receipts for that day were only a pound, all taken after six in the evening.

With heavy rent to pay, and other bills due for stock, lighting, rates, etc., the partners were forced to save money in every possible way. At first the two shared one room, in which they lived, paying *7s. 6d.* a week rent, but they had a spare room at the back of their shop, and for this they found a tenant who paid a similar sum as rent. As for food, one is driven to wonder how they managed at all, for Mr Gamage has put it on record that at first they could not allow themselves more than sixpence for their breakfast. Even though food was then half the price it is nowadays threepence seems a mighty small allowance for a man's breakfast. Certainly it did not run to bacon or even a kipper.

Another blow fell. Their seven-and-sixpenny tenant left, and since they were unable to find another they decided to use the room themselves, and, rigging it up as best they could, moved into it, and made it their home. Every penny spent was carefully accounted for, and their books show that, even after some months, when the business was beginning to get on its legs, Messrs Gamage and Spain spent only 14*s*. a week between them on their living. A shilling apiece daily for food is certainly cutting things rather close, and Mr Gamage has to thank the fine constitution which he inherited from his farmer ancestors for keeping his health under such trials.

The takings for the first year were £1632, for the second £1850, for the third £2300. A steady growth, but a slow one. One wonders whether Mr Gamage foresaw the time when the annual takings of his immense store would pass far beyond the million mark.

Soon after the Gamage shop was opened there was a sudden craze for hair-brushes with wire set in a pad of rubber, instead of the usual bristles. The standard price of these brushes was half a crown apiece, and at that price they were sold all over London. Imagine the horror and disgust of rivals when they saw the window of Gamage and Spain's little shop filled with these brushes marked at one and sixpence apiece. "Madness!" they said. "Crazy young fools headed straight for bankruptcy." But the public did not worry their heads about this point of view. They crowded in and swept the shop clear of brushes, and if there was not much profit on the brushes there was good profit in gaining new customers. "Gamage is satisfied with small profits," said an American wholesaler some years later. "That is the reason of his amazing success." The cheap sale of these brushes, instead of bankrupting the new firm, gave it new life, and was the first instance of the policy which its founder has pursued ever since.

Three busy years had passed when Mr Spain announced one day to his partner that he was engaged to be married. "And you will do the same one of these days, old chap," he said. "Now what are we to do, for it is quite plain that this business won't support two families? I think you had better buy me out, and I suggest that you pay me four hundred pounds."

When the partnership was first drawn up the two had agreed that if one or the other broke away the price paid should be left to arbitration. This was done, and Mr Spain received £425, or a little more than the sum for which he had asked.

It was a hard tussle, carrying on alone, but Mr Gamage never lost heart. Holborn was still a quiet street, but it was beginning to get more busy. Even in those days it was one of the main thoroughfares for people going to the City. Holborn Viaduct was opened so long ago as 1869, and Holborn Town Hall was in process of being built in the year when the Gamage shop was first opened. Mr Gamage set himself to catch customers by selling good articles at lower prices than they were sold elsewhere. This policy, while it pleased his customers, made him very unpopular with his rivals, who made many attempts to wreck his business.

But his biggest fights were with the manufacturers of proprietary articles, who demanded that he should sell at the standard prices which they imposed upon other retail houses. Mr Gamage pointed out to these manufacturers that by taking smaller profits they could immensely increase the sales of their goods, but they would have none of it. They fought him in every way, even in the Law Courts. But although they were the 'giants' and he merely a very small 'Jack' he managed to beat them, and steadily increased his business until, at the end of fifteen years, his shop was the largest in the neighbourhood.

The shop had been started, you will remember, purely as a hosiery establishment, but Mr Gamage had gradually increased his scope, and in the early 'nineties was already offering quite a variety of goods to his customers, and was always looking out for novelties. Then came the bicycle boom. London went quite mad on the new safety bicycle. Every one who could afford a machine rode. Men went to their offices on their bicycles, bicycle parties were given in the West End, and afterward the guests rode by night through the quiet streets of the City; bicycle shops sprang up everywhere, and cycle papers started and gained large circulation.

But bicycles were very expensive. Twelve and fifteen guineas were asked for machines by well-known makers, so once more Mr Gamage saw an opportunity and seized it. By contracting for a very large number of machines he secured a sound bicycle which he was able to sell at a price that defied competition. "Good goods and small profits" was his motto, and again he proved how well it paid by his enormous sales. Customers came in their hundreds for bicycles, and it was the success of this venture which gradually converted Gamages from a hosiery shop to the great games and sports depot which it has since become, which led to the purchase of Benetfinks in 1907, and which has made the great store the Mecca of young folk as well as of their parents.

By 1897 Gamages had become so large that its owner turned it into a Limited Liability Company, but he still retained control, and to-day his son, Mr Eric M. Gamage, remains in command of the huge business. The capital is £650,000, the yearly sales exceed a million, and more than two thousand people are employed in the great range of buildings on the north side of Holborn.

Mr Gamage himself has largely retired from business and gone back to the occupations of his youth, farming and gardening. He was always a lover of the country, and his career, like that of Mr Gordon Selfridge, proves how a country boy, with no other equipment than good health, ambition, and power of work, can make a great fortune and a great success.

Reading the story of a merchant prince like Mr Gamage, you are apt to think of him as simply a great brain, the centre of a huge money-making organization. Do not run away with any such idea, for Mr Gamage is a very human sort of person. He is very good to the people employed in his great store and very popular with them, and as for sticking in his office year after year, nothing could be further from the truth, for in pursuit of business he has travelled all over Europe and North America.

Once when in an Austrian town he saw a new toy in a shop window, which took his fancy, and he went in and bought it. He learned that the maker lived in a little town far off the beaten track of travel, and without losing a day started off to find him. It took him two whole days to reach and find the man, but he smiles with pleasure at the recollection that his was the only shop in England to secure a stock of this special toy.

On another occasion when in America he got upon the track of a new sort of toy gun, and at once started out to see the inventor. Here again the man lived in a remote village, and Mr Gamage found that he would have to drive many miles over a rough road in the depths of winter. He did not hesitate, but hired a buggy and started. A violent blizzard came on, the temperature fell to zero, and a gale drove finely powdered snow in blinding drifts. Most people would have given up and gone back, but not Mr Gamage. He carried on, arrived in a half-frozen condition, and secured a good stock of the novelty.

Gamages pride themselves on their service; they never like to fail a customer. Just before Christmas some years ago a lady visited the shop to buy a rocking-horse for her small son. Christmas Eve came, and to her dismay the rocking-horse had not arrived. Evening came, still no rocking-horse, and the lady found that the shop was shut. She opened the telephone directory, found Mr Gamage's private address, and telephoned to him direct. "It will be all right," was the answer. "Your son shall have his horse."

Very early next morning Mr Gamage got out his car and drove to Holborn. He unlocked the empty shop, got out the rocking-horse with his own hands, then, rigging himself up as Father Christmas, he drove on to the customer's address and personally delivered the gift. You can imagine for yourself the youngster's delight.

CHAPTER VIII

THE STEEL KING OF GREAT BRITAIN

Sir Robert A. Hadfield and his Story

YOU often hear the heads of the great northern engineering firms described as iron-masters, but Sir Robert Hadfield is more than an iron-master. He is a steel-king. He is the man to whom the great steel industry of the world—not of Britain only—owes a greater debt than to any other, since that unknown inventor who, thousands of years ago, turned soft iron into cutting steel by fusing it with charcoal. As the inventor of manganese steel he comes under the description of scientist rather than mere business man, yet as the head of one of the greatest iron- and steel-works in Britain he is certainly a king of commerce.

You might say that Sir Robert had iron in his blood, for his father, Mr Robert Hadfield, was a well-known iron-master and founder of the Attercliffe works which later became the famous Hecla Works of Hadfield's Ltd. Also he was born in Sheffield, the centre of the British steel industry.

Sheffield has made and still makes steel which is the best in the world. Steel-makers from other parts of the world have come to Sheffield to learn her secrets, and gone home to try to copy her steel, yet never succeeded in equalling its peculiar excellence. It is said that one foreign steel-manufacturer went so far as to import a number of barrels of Sheffield water in the belief that this was the secret of Sheffield's marvellous steel. Yet he, like the rest, was doomed to disappointment.

Though born in Sheffield, Sir Robert comes of an old Derbyshire yeoman family whose home is in Edale in the centre of the beautiful Peak District. Edale lies under the shadow of Kinderscout, the highest mountain in the Peak. Many famous writers have chosen this part of the world as the scene of their stories. It is described by Charlotte Brontë in *Jane Eyre,* by Mrs Humphry Ward in *David Grieve,* while Castleton, which is near by, was celebrated by Sir Walter Scott in *Peveril of the Peak.* Mam Tor, that queer hill called the Shivering Mountain, and the famous Blue John Mine are close to Edale, and so is the River Derwent, where Izaak Walton fished for trout. One of Sir Robert's ancestors, Major Hadfield, fought in the battle of Flodden, and his sword is still in the possession of the family.

Sir Robert's father lived in Sheffield, and for fourteen years was on the city council and chairman of the Highways Committee. He was one of the first steel-makers to begin the manufacture of large steel castings. Robert Junior went to the Sheffield Collegiate School.

In those days chemistry was very little taught at big schools. At the average Public School there was one hour a week of what was impolitely called 'stinks,' and hardly anyone took it seriously, except perhaps the unfortunate master. But Sheffield was an exception; the teaching was good, and young Hadfield was very keen on it, so much so that he had special tuition under a very clever tutor, the late Mr A. H. Allen. When the boy was sixteen his father asked him what he would like to do, whether he would go to a University or come straight into the business. Robert did not hesitate for a moment. He voted for the business, and in 1876, when just seventeen, entered the laboratory at his father's works. He plunged at once into research-work.

Very fine steel was being made in Sheffield even at that date, but there was practically only one method known—that invented by Bessemer in 1856, which consisted in passing cold air through liquid iron. It is true that tungsten steel had been made in Germany as early as 1859, but most steel-making was done by rule of thumb, and very little was known of the chemistry of the process.

Robert Hadfield set himself to investigate the influence of other metals on iron, and turned his attention specially to the influence of manganese in steel-making. Manganese is a metal belonging to the iron group, but is darker than wrought iron, and is one of the hardest metals known, so hard that it will scratch both steel and glass.

Twelve long years Robert Hadfield worked steadily, with the result that in 1888 he was able to read a paper before the Institute of Civil Engineers, in which he announced his discovery of manganese steel. He showed that this steel had properties of hardness far exceeding any steel yet made, and prophesied that it would come into use for all purposes requiring strength and hardness. He has lived to see his steel used for rock-crushing machinery, safes, railway switches, and—above all—for cutting-tools of an immense variety.

Speaking of the discovery of this steel, great scientists declared that it takes place with such scientific landmarks as Perkin's discovery of coal-tar dyes, or the invention of the basic process for the manufacture of steel.

Do not fancy, however, that young Hadfield spent his whole time in the laboratory. He was a man of affairs as well as a scientist, and very soon was his father's right-hand man in the management of the works. In 1888, when not yet thirty years of age, he became chairman and managing director of the whole business. At that time the hours of work were very long. Ten hours a day was quite usual in ironworks, and there was no Saturday half-holiday. In iron- and steel-making, the blast-furnaces, once lighted, have to be kept going, for it costs hundreds of pounds to relight a furnace once it has gone cold. Consequently shifts have to keep busy all Sunday, as well as other days. The new manager had long believed that the hours were too long, and in 1891 announced that no man in the firm's employ would work more than forty-eight hours a week. There was a tremendous outcry among other employers who bitterly resented this innovation by their young rival, but Robert stuck to his resolve, and very soon the others had to fall into line.

The men themselves never forgot their debt to Robert Hadfield, and strikes and lock-outs were unknown in his works. Until the general strike of 1921, when all iron-makers were forced to come out by their unions, Hadfield's never lost a day through labour troubles. It has been the practice of the firm to have a committee made up of masters and men and to submit all disputes to this board. By means of these conferences the relations between the firm and its people have always been of the happiest character. The firm has done a great deal for its people. Many years ago a canteen was established at the Hecla Works, but the heads of the firm have left its management entirely to the workpeople.

A committee of the men control the meals, prices, and everything, and the rooms are used for all sorts of social functions connected with the works. A sports ground of fourteen acres has been purchased by the firm, and this too is run by the men themselves.

Discoveries such as those of Robert Hadfield were not long in bringing rewards. In 1888 the Institute of Civil Engineers presented the young inventor with the splendid Telford gold medal for his discovery of manganese steel, and a few years later he received the George Stephenson gold medal for his researches in nickel-iron alloys. In 1903 the Howard prize and premium were his. This honour is given only once in five years. Since then he has the Bessemer gold medal from the Iron and Steel Institute and the James Forrest premium for lecturing. America honoured him by giving him the John Fritz gold medal, which has been presented to such great men as Edison, Lord Kelvin, and Westinghouse of brake fame, and is the highest gift of its kind in the United States. More recently he was elected a member of the American Academy of Sciences, a body which has 225 members, only nine of whom are of British nationality. He has had several gold medals from France, and has been elected a member of the Legion of Honour. In 1919 the city authorities of Boulogne voted him the Napoleon III bronze medal for the good work he had done for the St Louis Hospital of Boulogne. He was knighted in 1908, and nine years later made a baronet.

Speaking of what he did for France in the War, his own country owes him a still greater debt, for during the Great War more ammunition was made for the British Navy at Hadfield's than in the works of any other manufacturer. Almost equally large quantities were produced for the Army, and at one time no fewer than nine thousand 9.2 inch explosive shells were manufactured weekly at the Hadfield works. More than that, the manganese steel invented by Sir Robert and turned out in his works was found to be by far the best for the steel helmets which were worn not only by the army but also by special constables during air-raids, and which were so well known as 'tin hats.' No fewer than seven million helmets were made of this special steel for use by the English, American, and Belgian armies, and it is no exaggeration to say that thousands of lives were saved, and tens of thousands of bad head-wounds avoided by the use of these helmets.

The Hadfield hospital which Sir Robert and Lady Hadfield financed and managed was opened in 1914 at Wimereux near Boulogne, and was carried on all through the War. No fewer than sixteen thousand patients passed through it, and both the Prime Minister of England and the Secretary of War gave personal thanks to Sir Robert for maintaining this wonderful institution.

In spite of all his other activities Sir Robert has never ceased his research-work on the various alloys of iron with such metals as nickel, chromium, tungsten, molybdenum, and aluminium, and the greatest of his more recent discoveries has been what is called 'low hysteresis steel.' Professor Morton G. Lloyd, one of the greatest of America's electrical experts, has said: "Sir Robert Hadfield in England has experimented with a number of alloy steels and found that either aluminium or silicon would greatly improve the magnetic quality when introduced in a proportion of two or three per cent. Silicon has proved the most useful, industrially. . . . This low hysteresis steel is that now almost entirely used for transformer cores, and is made by several of the Hadfield licensees in this country (U.S.A.). . . . No other alloy steel has proved of such industrial importance as the Hadfield low hysteresis steel."

Another well-known American scientist, Mr T. D. Yensen, speaks in even stronger terms of the value of this new steel. In a paper written in 1921 he says: "The total saving already effected to the world by the Hadfield low hysteresis steel in reducing energy losses, saving in copper, better apparatus, and other advantages, amounts to no less than 340 million dollars (about £80,000,000 sterling), or nearly enough to build the Panama Canal." At the time of writing the value of this benefit must have been easily doubled. One more remark about Sir Robert, worth quoting, is from the lips of the late Andrew Carnegie, greatest of American iron-masters. "Hadfield," he said, on the occasion of the presentation of the Bessemer medal to Sir Robert, "Hadfield has achieved the rare distinction of being foremost in the line he has chosen. His position is not equalled in the world in this special line, and therefore we bow to him as a master among men."

Most men would be satisfied with such a combination as being head of a huge ironworks and a great inventor into the bargain, yet Sir Robert finds time to busy himself with other matters. He is particularly keen upon the improvement of railways, and for years past has been insisting that the best way to help trade is to bring down British railway rates, which rose more than 100 per cent. during the Great War. High rates, he urges, restrict traffic, and the companies would be better off with cheaper rates and an increased volume of traffic.

He believes too that much might be done by increasing

SIR ROBERT HADFIELD 96

Photo Elliott & Fry, Ltd.

the wagon capacity of British railways. In America each of the freight-cars or wagons weighs some twenty tons in itself, and carries an additional weight of forty-six tons, but the small wagons used on British railways carry on an average less than one-sixth of that weight. Sir Robert has the word of no less an authority than Sir Harry Thornton, formerly General Manager of the Great Eastern Railway, that there could be built and used in England wagons up to thirty or even forty tons capacity, and he is very anxious that the experiment should be tried.

On a visit to America he watched a most interesting experiment in heavy pulling. The test train was made up of one hundred loaded one-hundred-and-twenty-ton cars, with an observation car. An ordinary English passenger-train weighs, unloaded, about three hundred tons, but this tremendous train weighed more than twelve thousand. Five locomotives were required to start it out of the yard, but once it got going three engines were detached, leaving a pusher at the rear, and in front one of the heaviest and most powerful locomotives in the world, which, with its tender, weighed 401 tons. Presently the pusher was detached, and after the one big engine had worked the train down a slope ten more one-hundred-and-twenty-ton cars were attached, giving a total load of 15,400 tons. The train, it may be mentioned, was a mile and one-sixteenth long, and was hauled by one engine over two hundred and fifty level miles of line. This, says Sir Robert, is a world's record, and though Britain cannot hope to equal it there is no real reason why she should not make some attempt to do so.

It has been mentioned that Sir Robert Hadfield was

awarded the James Forrest premium for lecturing. When you hear that between 1888 and 1922 he wrote and read no fewer than one hundred and thirty-five papers you will agree that he deserved it. Looking through a list of these lectures, you find that Sir Robert is an authority on every form of iron and steel, iron ores, and iron's diseases. One paper deals entirely with corrosion and rust, another with fuels, a third with education, and a fourth with X-ray examinations of iron and steel. There are few more many-sided men among our kings of commerce than the subject of this chapter.

CHAPTER IX

FROM *ANSWERS* TO *THE TIMES*

The Romance of the Harmsworths

OF all the romances of business success there is none more dramatic than the story of the two Harmsworth brothers—one of whom became Lord Northcliffe, the greatest journalist Britain has ever known, and the other Lord Rothermere, one of the greatest business men of our generation.

The story of their amazing rise to fame begins when, as boys, they became enthusiastic about the joys of the bicycle, then only just invented.

In those days the bicycle offered the town-dweller the opportunity of getting speedily into the country at week-ends and when his daily work was done. Alfred Harmsworth, interested from boyhood in every new idea, became the central figure in a group of bicyclists who used to sally forth from St John's Wood at week-ends in search of fresh air and such adventures as were to be found on the open road in those days.

Another boy who knew the two Harmsworths—Alfred and Harold—in those boyhood days, Sir Max Pemberton, gives a glimpse of the way the week-ends were spent in his book on Lord Northcliffe :

> Ripley was at that time a truly primitive village. I do not know which of the pioneers among us was the first to discover it ; but discover it we certainly did, and at the Anchor Inn

we spent the best part of many a week-end. Soon the place became a bicycling fashion. There would be forty or fifty riders at lunch at the Anchor every Saturday ; and from being a mere alehouse, the thing became a highly prosperous concern. To reach it by lunchtime we had to leave St John's Wood before nine o'clock in the morning, for we had a run of more than thirty miles to make ; and having spent the day in often hopeless attempts to extract fish from the River Wey, we would leave at five or six in the afternoon and reach St John's Wood about ten o'clock.

And here is a picture by the same writer of the more famous of the two Harmsworths, which shows that Lord Northcliffe was very much like the average healthy boy :

Alfred Harmsworth was always the life of these pilgrimages. He had many friends and certainly no enemies as a boy. I should describe him then as given to high spirits but never to elation. He had a romantic bias, but added to romance a most practical temperament. He was staunch in friendship but exceedingly well able to take care of himself when the other cheek was not offered. Indeed, there were few boys who did not envy him.

The father of these two boys was a distinguished barrister, and both Mr and Mrs Harmsworth hoped that their son Alfred would ' follow in father's footsteps ' and become a lawyer. It was not to be. Even at school the budding Northcliffe had dabbled in printer's ink as the editor of the school magazine, and after completing his education his thoughts centred upon the great problem of becoming a real journalist.

And it was a great problem in those early years, for the newspapers were then stately productions written by experts, and the great army of popular periodicals and boys' papers which sell by the million copies to-day did not then exist.

It was precisely this fact that gave Alfred Harmsworth his great chance. He thought that popular reading for all classes ought to exist—that as free education had been introduced, and every one was being taught to read, some one ought to provide this great new public with bright, interesting reading-matter, and the success of *Tit-Bits*, started by George Newnes, only made him more sure than ever that he was right.

George Augustus Sala, the great editor of *The Daily Telegraph*, warned young Harmsworth against entering journalism. It was, said Mr Sala, a precarious career at the best of times, and just then, when the public was changing so rapidly, it was more precarious than ever.

If Alfred Harmsworth had taken that advice the world would never have known a Lord Northcliffe, and probably no Lord Rothermere either, for the brothers rose to fame together. Fortunately for journalism Alfred Harmsworth knew his own mind, and the sure judgment which in later years enabled him to found the *Daily Mail* just when it was wanted, and caused him to offer huge prizes to help aviation in its first years, came to his rescue. He decided that whatever anyone said he would be a journalist.

He began his amazing career as a free-lance writer at the age of sixteen, and a year later secured his first staff appointment as the assistant-editor of a boys' paper called *Youth* at the magnificent salary of 31*s.* 6*d.* per week.

The paper was a failure, and even the brains of the seventeen-year-old boy who was destined to start so many successful journals did not save it. A year later he was free-lancing again, still determined, in spite of this early piece of ill-luck, to make his name as an editor.

It is surprising in how many cases men have, by perseverance, turned early failures into brilliant successes. Alfred Harmsworth was only one of many, but in his case he had to fight ill-health as well. As a boy he was not strong, and many of his friends urged him to find work of a less worrying nature than trying to sell articles in Fleet Street.

Thus Alfred Harmsworth faced the turning-point in his life before the age of twenty, and he met it with an outward thrust of his strong chin and a determination to struggle on until he got the chance which he always believed would come to him. Had he thought only of earning money he could have taken many positions offering more pay than journalism. Had he thought of an easy time he could have got it by entering the office of one of his mother's business friends. But he wanted success, made by his own efforts, along the lines he had planned, and he risked everything to achieve it. Alfred Harmsworth is a striking example of the fact that it is all-important for every boy to decide what he wishes to make of his life, and then to work hard to gain his goal.

He secured a position with a firm of publishers at Coventry, where he learned all he could about printing and the technical side of producing a paper.

By the time he was twenty-three he had returned to London and begun his great career as the part proprietor of a business which produced cheap books such as *All about our Railways*. His partner in this firm, a Mr Carr, talked over with him Alfred Harmsworth's great project of a weekly paper for every one, and, impressed by the young man's enthusiasm, he offered to provide some of the capital necessary to start it. Finding that Mr James Henderson, the head of another publishing house for whom he had written many articles in the past, also believed that success was possible, Alfred Harmsworth decided to launch his first paper under the title of *Answers to Correspondents.* Thus it came about that almost exactly forty years ago, on June 2, 1888, Alfred Harmsworth sat in a tiny room at 26 Paternoster Square and turned over the pages of the first issue of what has since become Britain's most famous weekly paper under the shorter title of *Answers.*

The idea of *Answers,* as described by the future Lord Northcliffe in the first number, was " to answer questions addressed to us. We shall answer all private matters by post. If, on the other hand, you ask us a question on a really interesting subject we shall ' pop ' the answer into our paper, which will in a week or two consist mainly of replies to correspondents."

That same first issue contained articles upon such interesting topics as " Silk Stockings," and " How to live on Nothing a Year."

It is commonly thought to-day, because of the great successes which the brothers Harmsworth were to achieve in later years, that *Answers* was an immediate success. This was not so. The circulation of that first issue was only 12,000 copies, and it was produced at a loss. Sales were mainly confined to London, and the growth of readers in the Provinces was a slow process.

After the months of breathless preparation and effort this was a disappointing result, and there were some who prophesied that *Answers* was doomed to fizzle out as a failure. The young man who had planned it and became its first editor did not think about such things. He meant it to succeed, and his time was taken up in planning fresh issues which would make the public buy it.

Working in his shirt-sleeves, with his one tiny office divided into two rooms, one the 'editorial office' and the other the 'publishing department,' he struggled with the task of deciding which of the hundreds of ideas that whirled through his quick brain would increase the circulation before his capital had disappeared.

A friend of the writers has told them of the 'christening-party,' consisting of a few friends, who were invited into that office to commemorate the publication of the first number.

It was June, and the strawberry season, and Alfred and Harold Harmsworth were the hosts. But the number of friends who would turn up, or perhaps their appetite for strawberries, had been misjudged, and in the middle of that tea-party it was found necessary for Harold Harmsworth to run out and buy another two pounds of the fruit from a street seller in Ludgate Hill.

A simple story, but how typical of the enthusiasm which Alfred Harmsworth showed for all his enterprises—that christening-party to celebrate a paper which every one thought would fail but the two brothers who had light-heartedly entered upon their great careers.

In the first number a prize of one guinea was offered for the best joke submitted on a postcard, a feature which has been retained in the paper until this day. In the second issue a more ambitious prize offer of a fortnight on the Continent was announced for the reader sending in the best list of suggestions for competitions.

In three months the editor, who had never for an

instant doubted the issue, had steered the new paper to success. By September 1888 *Answers* was no longer losing money, and the circulation was slowly rising.

It was at this point that Harold Harmsworth, the future Lord Rothermere, made his courageous decision to throw up a good position in the Civil Service and join his brother as business manager. Harold Harmsworth had left school with the reputation of being a brilliant mathematician, and his experience in the Board of Trade had taught him all there was to be known about figures. Within a few months of joining his brother the balance sheet of the new paper was showing a net profit of two thousand pounds a year. Harold Harmsworth had a mind as steady as his brother's was brilliant, and his sober judgment helped to prevent the mistakes which sometimes arise from misplaced enthusiasm. It was an admirable combination, destined to do great things in Fleet Street, and by the end of the first year these two young men, who in those days were both regarded as being too young to control such a business by many people, had raised the paper to an average weekly circulation of nearly 50,000 copies.

Lord Northcliffe's career proved the large part which ideas—your own ideas—can play in building up a career. Hardly a week passed in those early days without some new offer appearing in *Answers*, designed to make people talk about the new paper.

Very early he had included a free insurance for readers against death or disablement in railway accidents. But it was in October 1889 that Alfred Harmsworth brought off his first big scoop. In that month he offered in *Answers* the then unheard-of prize of £1 a week for life to the reader making the nearest guess to the total amount of gold and silver in the Bank of England on December 4 of that year.

For two months following this announcement millions talked of little else. This one idea brought Alfred Harmsworth his first fame. Many thought that such a huge prize would involve the paper in a heavy loss, but the Harmsworths knew better. When the competition closed 718,000 postcards had been received, which meant that that number of people had bought *Answers* to read the conditions of the contest.

A touch of the Harmsworth genius was added by the rule that each postcard must be witnessed by five people, which meant that over four million people had had *Answers* brought directly to their notice.

Those days of first success were exciting times at 108 Fleet Street, the larger offices to which the paper had moved. While Alfred Harmsworth produced new issues and watched the thousands of entries arriving, Harold, his brother, sat in the publishing department, listening to orders for " more *Answers* " pouring over the telephone-wires, which meant increasing the printing orders daily.

The prize was won by a soldier in the Ordnance Survey Department, whose guess was within £2 of the correct amount ; and by the time the sensation of this competition had died down the paper had a circulation of over 350,000 copies a week.

The time had now come when the Harmsworths were sufficiently strongly established to think about starting other papers. After studying the prospects carefully they decided to put on the market a halfpenny comic paper called *Comic Cuts*. Older journalists, remembering that no humorous paper had ever been sold at less than one penny, said that it could not be done, but the coming of *Comic Cuts* proved once more that the Harmsworths were right, and their critics wrong, for the new paper made a profit of over £20,000 a year from the start.

Alfred Harmsworth was now becoming wealthy enough, thanks to his brother's policy of putting the profits back into the business, to develop those other ideas of which he had dreamt while bicycling along the Ripley Road as a boy. *Comic Cuts* was followed by *Forget-Me-Not*, a woman's weekly paper, and a second and third paper of a humorous nature. These were followed by the *Sunday Companion* and the *Sunday Circle*, and so was built up the great organization which, beginning in one room at Paternoster Square, became Answers Ltd. in 1893, and is to-day known as the Amalgamated Press Ltd.

Within five years of the first issue of *Answers* the Harmsworths owned their own printing works, which grew into a group of the largest printing works in the country at Southwark and Gravesend.

Amid all the other interests of his later life, of which we are about to write, Lord Northcliffe retained his interest in the organization he had created during those youthful years, until he had seen it develop into the greatest publishing business in the world, handling over a hundred different publications, with one person in every four of our entire population buying at least one of those papers every week.

In the year of Lord Northcliffe's death this great firm, founded by his vision and guided through its early years by the genius of Alfred and Harold Harmsworth, employed eight hundred persons on the editorial and commercial staffs alone, and was paying out £5500 a week to authors and artists. To print its papers needed 35,000 tons of paper a year, and those papers were advertised in every corner of the country by no fewer than twelve million posters. All created by two young men who clung to one idea—the idea that the boys and girls who were being taught to read would be glad to buy papers which gave them informative articles in an interesting form.

It was in the year 1896, when the *Answers* company had been rechristened Harmsworth Brothers Ltd., that the two Harmsworths, now wealthy men, entered the newspaper market.

In spite of Alfred Harmsworth's enormous success in the field of weekly papers many expert journalists shook their heads sadly when they learnt that these two young men, in co-operation with a Mr Kennedy Jones, then acting editor of the *Sun* newspaper, had bought the *Evening News*.

The *Evening News* had been losing money for many years, and most people imagined that the paper would go on losing money whatever Alfred Harmsworth might do. What the experts did not know, for the Harmsworths did not talk about their plans, was that the purchase of this newspaper for £25,000 was the first step in a great plan for founding a popular halfpenny morning newspaper, which Alfred Harmsworth had planned while employed at Coventry years before.

Having bought the paper, the brothers proceeded to 'try out' their ideas. They worked. The *Evening News* circulation began to grow, and went on growing.

Meanwhile, under the cloak of the utmost secrecy, their real task of founding the *Daily Mail* went steadily ahead. For months before May 4, the date selected for the publication of the first issue, complete trial copies were printed. It was typical of Alfred Harmsworth's 'staff work' that certain copies, filled with grotesque features, got into other hands—and convinced those who saw them that the new paper, if it ever appeared, was doomed to an early death.

The story of that memorable first issue of the paper which will be remembered for all time as Lord Northcliffe's greatest success may best be described in his own words, spoken on the twentieth anniversary of its birth:

> While the project of a complete morning newspaper at a halfpenny aroused comparatively little interest among those most directly concerned (the proprietors of the penny morning newspapers and the owners of *The Times*, which had maintained its price of threepence since 1861), events proved that the public was vastly interested at the new development, and far more so than we anticipated. We had prepared for an issue of one hundred thousand copies. The paper chosen was, as now, exactly that used by penny morning newspapers. We were equipped with the very latest in mechanical appliances. Able young men from everywhere, having watched the progress of the *Evening News*, were offering their services. We thought that we had made every provision for every contingency, but the only lack of foresight shown, if I may say so with modesty, was in not anticipating the immense demand which resulted. The actual number of copies produced on the first day was three hundred and ninety-seven thousand two hundred and fifteen, and it became instantly necessary to commandeer various neighbouring printing establishments while more machinery was being made for us.

Sir Max Pemberton tells us, in his life of Lord Northcliffe, how Alfred Harmsworth did not leave his office for the first two days and nights after the new paper appeared. When he returned at last to his house in Berkeley Square, he slept for twenty-two hours continuously, greatly alarming the household. Thus did Alfred Harmsworth find himself, at the age of thirty-five, the chief proprietor of a string of weekly periodicals and the inspiring genius of the *Daily Mail*, now four years old and already with a circulation of from 750,000 to one million copies daily. Such success as this had never been heard of before, least of all such success coming to two journalists—for Harold Harmsworth remained the business head of the concerns—who were still little more than boys. Actually this story of the greatest journalist of our generation is striking evidence that the dreams of the boy are often so instinctively sound that they will lead him to the greatest opportunity of his life. Alfred Harmsworth did not wait for something to turn up—he knew what he wanted to do at sixteen, and twenty years later he had carried those plans through to brilliant success.

The Harmsworths were making money—and they also believed in spending it. No expense was spared where their papers were concerned. Special correspondents were sent to the ends of the earth if a good story was likely to be obtained. There is on record a cabled account of an earthquake in Martinique, about a column long, which cost a thousand pounds. This was the price which the Harmsworths paid to make the *Daily Mail* the most progressive paper in the country.

We have mentioned that Alfred Harmsworth had to battle with ill-health as a boy. All through his life he had to remember that illness was the penalty of doing too much. In the height of his career he still went to bed at nine o'clock nearly every night, rising at six in the morning to go through all the morning papers. Within a month or two of his death he was staying at his country house, and rising at this early hour, to go through all the papers in the open air, "to make sure that we haven't missed anything." Thoroughness and perseverance, these two qualities allied to brilliance in ideas stand out above all other qualities in him.

With the founding of the *Daily Mail* and the growth of the Amalgamated Press into the greatest publishing business in the world the creative part of this great career was complete. That career he crowned by the spectacular action of buying *The Times*. For a short time the greatest of all British newspapers was owned by the greatest of all British journalists. The little boy who planned big things while cycling along the Ripley Road had now been recognized by all as the master-mind of Fleet Street.

Before this his great services to his country—for the Harmsworths had always been staunch patriots and they used all their papers to preach the glories of the Empire and the great work for civilization which our commonwealth of nations is doing—had been recognized by a baronetcy in 1904 and then, two years later, by a peerage. Shortly afterwards Harold Harmsworth also joined the peerage as Lord Rothermere, a well-deserved tribute to his organizing genius.

There is no room here to tell of the other great episodes in their careers, which must, however, be mentioned. There was the founding of the *Daily Mirror*, first a failure as purely a woman's daily paper, and then converted into a brilliant success as the first picture newspaper. And a word must be added about the War activities of the Harmsworths, which were so valuable that many people declared that "it was Lloyd George and Northcliffe who won the War for Britain."

Those who gave the great journalist such extravagant praise were probably thinking of Lord Northcliffe's work as the spokesman of the British War Mission to the United States in 1917. America had just entered the conflict, and it was Northcliffe's task to explain the issues so vividly that the whole resources of the great Western Republic should be mobilized freely and expeditiously to assist the hard-pressed Allied armies on the western front.

Into this task he threw the whole of his enormous energy. He had agreed to spend three months in the United States, he actually spent six months there. Upon one occasion he was twenty-one days in a train, travelling from the Canadian border to the extreme south, eloquently stating the truth about the War at every stopping-place. It was a great work for the Allied cause, for which his countrymen owed him much.

While Lord Northcliffe was heartening the country through his papers, and himself doing the work of a dozen men for the cause, Lord Rothermere was working equally hard for victory, for a time as Air Minister, and later in other ways.

There was something particularly fitting in the presence of one of the Harmsworth brothers at the newly-formed Air Ministry at the crisis of the War, for no two men had done so much to encourage flying in its early years as these two journalists.

Lord Northcliffe particularly had always been fond of machines. We have spoken of his love of bicycling in its earliest days. When motor-cycling came he took to that with equal zest, and in 1895 he had ridden one of the new motor-cycles in France. The machine ran away with him, leapt a hedge, and landed him in a field. But that did not damp his ardour, and when the motor arrived he and his brother were among the first to realize

LORD NORTHCLIFFE

that the new machine was destined to oust the horse and revolutionize not only transport but the habits of the people.

He bought one of the first motor-cars ever made, and as they were improved he became the owner of each new model, always driving himself. In the last year of his life he expressed his own wants to Sir Max Pemberton in these words: "A car and a telephone and a good bed—what more do I want?"

When, during a visit to the United States before the War, this man with the mind of eternal youth first heard of the brothers Wright and their first flight in a heavier-than-air machine he turned his restless brain to the problem of flight, and in the *Daily Mail* he offered a prize of £10,000 for the first mechanical flight from London to Manchester in twenty-four hours, with not more than two stops.

Most people regarded aviation as a fad which would die out. Northcliffe and his brother knew better. He followed up this offer by another of £1000 for the first man to fly across the Channel. It was won by M. Blériot, who crossed the narrow straits on July 25, 1909, in thirty-seven minutes. When, on April 28, 1910, the £10,000 prize for a London to Manchester flight was won by M. Paulhan the world realized that the Harmsworths were not so mad after all, and that man had at last conquered the air.

The War strain affected the health of a man who had never been robust, and upon Lord Northcliffe's return from his famous world tour it was evident that only prolonged rest could restore his powers. And the tragedy of one of the most romantic careers of our generation was that he could not rest. He went off again, this time into Germany to see that country for himself after the great defeat, and he returned home to die.

After his death Lord Rothermere became the chief owner of all his newspaper interests, including the *Daily Mail* and the *Daily Mirror*. Of the newspapers he controlled only *The Times* left the Harmsworth family, to be bought in trust for the nation and never offered for sale again.

To-day Harold Harmsworth, the business brain behind the family fortunes from those first weeks of *Answers*, remains the biggest newspaper proprietor in the country. As we write, a new chapter in the story of British journalism is being opened by the announcement that the successor to Alfred Harmsworth is about to found a string of evening journals in British provincial cities. And it seems natural that the great business built up by Lord Northcliffe should not stand still.

In Tudor Street, just off Fleet Street, you will find a giant corner building, the most perfectly equipped newspaper works in the world. Over the door is its name, " Northcliffe House." It is the most appropriate memorial that could have been erected to the memory of the editor of the school magazine who earned world-wide fame by his great idea of giving people interesting reading—the idea which made him the greatest journalist the world has ever seen.

CHAPTER X

FROM HALF-TIMER TO FINANCIER

The Romance of Sir Enoch Hill

SOME of our readers may not have heard of Sir Enoch Hill. He has never invented anything which has revolutionized the life of the masses. Nor has he ever laid the foundation of a fortune by any 'lucky strike,' or by speculating with a few pounds and turning them into thousands. If he ever had any dreams —and most successful men have—then they were of hard work and a useful life, rather than of fame and fortune.

The story of Sir Enoch Hill is the story of a poor English lad, who, starting life with no social advantages, precious little education, but immense industry and ambition, has become a great financier and the controlling hand of Britain's largest building society, with assets amounting to over £47,000,000.

Judging purely by the money he has made, Sir Enoch Hill has made no particular success in life. As far as we know, he is still poor compared with some of those fabulously wealthy men whose stories appear in these pages. Certainly Enoch Hill is not a millionaire, for the very good reason that he has no desire to be one. His desire from the first was to live a useful life, and to render helpful service to his fellow-men. How far he has achieved that ambition is revealed by the following newspaper report of a speech made by Sir Kingsley

Wood, M.P., Parliamentary Secretary to the Ministry of Health, at the last annual general meeting of the Halifax Building Society, the organization which for twenty-five years has expanded under his guidance :

> Sir Kingsley Wood referred to the unique service which Mr Hill had undoubtedly rendered to the nation. Few men had rendered in this generation such valuable services to the community as the managing director of that great society had done, and none could look back upon his public life with more satisfaction than Mr Hill could in having brought great happiness and great comfort to a large section of the community and in having at the same time built up a safe, stable, and reliable national institution.

That was a striking tribute to be publicly conferred upon one who had been a ' half-timer ' in a silk mill when he ought to have been learning to read and write. And since that speech an even greater tribute has been bestowed upon Enoch Hill—the honour of knighthood. These are tributes made possible only by the years of steady perseverance and industry which separated that ' half-timer ' from the General Manager of the greatest British Building Society.

The romance of Sir Enoch Hill is more than a story of dreams come true, however. It is a story which should inspire every boy who reads it, because this remarkable man never had one single advantage which is not possessed by the poorest boy in the land to-day. The most stimulating thing about the story is the fact that any boy can follow the same road, use the same methods, and if the character is there, gain the same respect and devotion of those he has served.

Enoch Hill was born at Leek, not far from the Potteries, sixty-two years ago. His parents were poor, like the majority of their neighbours at that time. Enoch was the eldest of a family of six, and at the age of eight his greatest desire was to contribute something toward the expenses of his home.

Tell anyone you want to be a financier, and you will be informed that you must study the higher mathematics, learn all about the laws of economics and the science of money, read everything you can upon such subjects as banking and currency, and obtain a junior position in a bank or office after completing your education.

Enoch Hill had as much chance of studying higher mathematics during early boyhood as has a cow of jumping over the moon. He took his first step up the ladder of success by obtaining work as the turner of a large wheel which supplied the motive power for a number of silk-winding frames.

He was a 'half-timer' while engaged in this work, and his wages for four and a half hours a day were 1*s*. a week. Education was compulsory, and young Hill was supposed to spend half of each week-day at school and the other half in the factory. But in those days it was possible, by attending school for one half-day a week, to secure a certificate of regular attendance during the remainder of the week. He took advantage of these slack conditions, and got precious little schooling of any sort in consequence.

Shortly after starting work he found a better position as a carrier of bobbins in a silk mill. From this post he progressed to the best job that was then open to 'half-timers'—the much-sought-after job of helper in a silk-twisting shed. It was hard work for small pay, but it taught him the value of money and it enabled a proud boy to take home his earnings at the end of the week.

After that for a short time the future General Manager of the Halifax Building Society worked as a farm-labourer, but quite naturally he quickly decided that this was not the work he wanted to do, and came back to the town to sell newspapers.

For some reason there are many famous men who claim to have begun life by selling newspapers, and of at least two men whose names are known and honoured by thousands to-day the statement is true. Those two men are Edgar Wallace and Enoch Hill.

Selling newspapers brought Enoch Hill into touch with the printing business, and before long he had secured work as a printer's 'devil' or assistant. Real progress now began. He got the chance of working overtime on Friday evenings, and often through the night, helping to print the local newspaper. This was done on an old-fashioned hand-press, at the rate of 100 copies per hour. To the boy who wanted to learn things there was something magical about that work—seeing the local news set up in type, and then watching it come off the press in the form of copies of the paper.

He became a compositor, and then a machine-hand. Still making headway, he got work in a general printing, bookbinding, and bookselling firm. He was getting on. Already he possessed the finest capital in the world—a reputation as a keen, industrious, and enthusiastic worker. But lack of education was still the stumbling-block.

At this point in his career Enoch Hill attracted the friendly help of the local vicar, who took an interest in him and coached him in reading, writing, and arithmetic.

This tuition was followed by the happy day when, after rendering slight services, which brought in extra sixpences, for the master of the grammar school, he received the offer of further guidance in arithmetic, grammar, and other subjects from the master.

Largely owing to the helping hands of these two worthy men, and the avidity with which Hill seized the opportunities thus brought within his reach, he secured a junior post with the Leek United Building Society. From that moment began Enoch Hill's connexion with the great social movement of which he is to-day one of the great authorities.

The young man was making what to him must have seemed like marvellous progress, but still he was not satisfied. He had secured a smattering of education, but not enough. So he continued to fit himself for bigger things by the only method he knew—tireless industry.

> And he while his companions slept
> Was toiling upward through the night.

He continued home studies, and without tuition learnt to write shorthand. Armed with this qualification, he became the sole contributor of local news for the north of Staffordshire to the *Staffordshire Advertiser*. By this time he had established a small commercial printing and bookselling business, so that he was doing three jobs at once, and learning something fresh out of each of them.

In 1900 he began his public life by becoming a member of the Technical and Secondary Education Committee of the local town council, representing the printing trades. Some local trade-unionists objected to this appointment because Enoch Hill, according to them, had not completed his education as a printer. In other words, because he had not completed the recognized apprenticeship.

Such a challenge was just what he wanted. He applied to the Guild of London for permission to sit, as an untrained student, for the examination in typography held by the Guild in connexion with the Manchester Technical School. This was granted, and he passed the technical test, although 40 per cent. of the trained entrants failed at that same examination! After that no more was heard about Enoch Hill's being an amateur.

He had been elected a member of the local council a year before, and had some years before been appointed a lay reader of the Church of England by the Bishop of Lichfield. In this office he did a great deal of helpful work for local churches, particularly in helping clergy during absences on holidays. Often he conducted services at three different churches in one day, a task which entailed sometimes walking twenty miles between sunrise and sunset during his one day of rest. Thus did this remarkable man repay the debt which he owed to the Church for that early help given him by the local vicar.

At about this time he secured a controlling interest in the Leek local paper, with which he is still associated to this day. That interest might have carried his footsteps into journalism, but for the fact that in 1896 he was appointed manager of the Leek United Building Society. He had to choose between the two interests, and the building society won. From that time he devoted all his efforts to the task of making easier the path of any man who wished to own his house.

During the next few years he more than doubled the operations of that society, and in 1902 there came to him the greatest chance of all.

In that year a vacancy occurred for a manager of the Halifax Permanent Building Society, even then one of the largest and most wealthy Building Societies in the world. He applied for the post and was selected out of 300 applicants.

To enable the reader to appreciate the qualifications required of the man who directs one of these great organizations some details of the romance of the Halifax Permanent Building Society must be given, if only because the story of this society during the past twenty-five years is the story of Enoch Hill himself.

It was on December 23, 1852 that the Halifax Permanent Building Society was really founded. The first office was in an upstairs room in Old Market, and the rent was ten pounds a year. One director, a steward, and the secretary attended each meeting at which subscriptions were paid by members. The director in attendance received sixpence for the first half-hour, one shilling for the second half-hour, and was fined two shillings for non-attendance.

In the course of a few months it became necessary to open the office daily from ten until four o'clock, and at the first annual meeting the directors were able to report that the receipts during the first year had amounted to £11,333 1s. 8*d*., and the balance showed a margin of assets over liabilities of £174 9*s*. 1*d*.

During the meeting one of the trustees delivered an address which may well be studied by those on the threshold of life to-day. In the course of this the speaker said :

> The Society has for its object the introduction of two principles, alike important to the peer and peasant, without which neither can flourish, viz., economy and systematic arrangement.

The first penny dropped into the thrift box by the boy, the shilling saved by the operative, and the pound or twenty pounds by the man in higher life, not infrequently forms his future character. So with system: the man who has his plans arranged, and his time marked out, finds his labour easy: whereas, when he acts in a contrary manner, everything runs into confusion. It would be taking the question in too unworthv a light to view it only according to the abstract principle of hoarding money, for it involves all the moral virtues. It produces not only independence, but also enterprise, liberality, and patriotism. You have selected for your title "The Halifax Permanent Benefit Building Society" and I trust the Society will be permanent in ages to come.

So permanent did that society continue to be that in 1882, thirty years later, it proudly announced that its assets were "over one million sterling."

When Mr Enoch Hill was appointed manager in 1902 the assets had grown to £1,500,000, with a membership of 8549 and an annual income of £559,000.

Twenty-five years pass, during which the "Halifax Permanent" has been guided from success to success by this remarkable financial authority who began life as a 'half-timer,' and we find that in 1928 the assets of the combined Halifax Permanent and Halifax Equitable Building Societies, merged together under the title of the Halifax Building Society under the continued management of Mr Hill, reach the astounding total of more than £47,000,000, the whole of which sum represents the savings of the thrifty.

The income of the Halifax Building Society, the largest in the world, for 1927, was £20,560,350 3*s*. 9*d*., and the number of new accounts opened during the year was 65,076, making a total of 257,248 persons who had at that date entrusted their savings to this

SIR ENOCH HILL *Photo L. N. A.*

great organization or utilized its facilities to buy homes for themselves.

In the strong rooms in the basement of "Permanent Buildings" in Halifax, the headquarters of the society, guarded by a steel *grille* and heavy steel fireproof doors, are thousands of deed boxes containing some seventy-five thousand parcels of deeds—records of ownership of houses which the society has helped to purchase. Every one of those deeds represents happiness and independence for some family in this country. And how many of them might not have realized what the Building Society offers but for the energy and enthusiasm which Enoch Hill has expended during the past quarter of a century in making these societies better known?

To come back to the man who is introduced at the beginning of this chapter as a poor boy, Sir Enoch Hill has done many other things during those strenuous years. He is interested in banking, in insurance, in accountancy. Since 1906 he has been a Fellow of the Chartered Institute of Secretaries. He has been chairman for some years of the Building Societies Association. He has in three elections been a candidate for Parliament and travelled widely abroad. During the War he helped the Government to raise loans to the extent of £3,000,000.

To-day, at the age of sixty-two, he is working harder than ever. You can usually find him at his desk by nine in the morning, and conferences, the business of the day, and perhaps a train journey to London where more business awaits him often mean a fourteen-hour day. Through it all he is happy, for this was the work that he has always wanted to do—and keep doing.

One of the very few things which annoys him is when a young man, on the threshold of life, complains that there is no chance in the world for the boy who has not had an expensive education.

Sir Enoch's advice to young men beginning life under great difficulties and hardship is not to be dismayed because all these can be overcome by industry and an endeavour to learn and 'get on,' and, he would add, "life for me has been interesting, fruitful, and happy. Do not worry, keep working and trying to please others, and all will be well."

And if the young man is wise he will remember the 'half-timer' in the silk mill, remember the lad teaching himself shorthand in the evenings, and then remember the Halifax Building Society with assets of over £47,000,000 and nearly 350,000 working accounts. What better example has ever existed of the fact that every man can make what he will of his own career?

CHAPTER XI

CARRYING THE FLAG FROM THE BOTTOM OF THE LADDER

Sir Hugo Hirst and his Story

"I WAS a very ordinary boy," is the rather surprising way in which Sir Hugo Hirst, founder and head of the greatest electrical company in existence, begins his story. "Boys who read about men who have achieved something out of the usual are apt to think that they are abnormal, but here they make a very great mistake. I liked athletics very much, and luckily was good at them. I did less homework than the other boys at my school, but paid more attention during school hours. This concentrated attention was appreciated by all the masters except one, who always used to recite his lecture which was taken down in shorthand by the class. I was the only one who sat bolt upright, while the others were industriously bent over their task. That put him off, and he disliked me in consequence.

"I had a good memory, and by my father's advice trained it in every way I could by learning poetry, by memorizing figures; and this training has helped me enormously and stood me in good stead throughout my life. I have learned since then that nothing one learns is ever lost, and that a use comes sooner or later for every piece of knowledge."

In the case of young Hirst it was not arithmetic, history, or accounts that brought him specially to the notice of his first employer. It was due rather to his outside knowledge—to languages, shorthand, and familiarity with the Morse code. Shorthand was not usual in those days, and he found it very valuable. His knowledge of Morse became useful in rather a curious way. The firm with which he was first employed had business connexions with foreign countries, and cables went to and fro constantly. Often messages of a hundred words or more would arrive, with possibly twenty words out of the hundred which could not be deciphered. In such a case it had been the custom of the firm to recable for confirmation of these words. The young clerk's knowledge enabled him to decipher these difficult words, and naturally saved the firm a good deal of money.

Yet this was not so great an advantage as might have been supposed, for the result was that he became amanuensis to the head of the firm, but without any extra pay, and at the same time the other clerks in the office grew jealous because he got a great deal of work over their heads. After a time he felt so unhappy that he looked about for fresh work, which he found with the Electric Power Storage Company, a London company formed to develop the use of secondary batteries.

Sir Hugo's father was a distiller, and the boy had studied chemistry for two years, in order to enter the business. He found this experience extremely useful while working for a firm which was making the first accumulators. While he was with this company Sir Hugo had several amusing experiences. When going up the Thames from Millwall to Westminster in the very first electrically driven launch then on the river an old skipper leaned over the side of his barge and stared in amazement at the new-fangled craft. " 'Ere, guv'nor," he shouted at last, " where's yer funnel ? "

Motor-cars were as little known in those days as motor-boats, and there was great excitement when an electrically propelled dog-cart was made ready for testing. The route chosen for the test was from Blackfriars Bridge to Westminster, but in those days every mechanically propelled vehicle was treated like a steam-roller, and a man had to walk in front of it with a red flag when it was going. Sir Hugo, being well known to the heads of his firm as a footballer and runner, was chosen for the job of running in front of the car, carrying the flag.

His life at that time was full of hard work, and some of that work was in the shops of the factory at Millwall, places dirty, dingy, and depressing beyond belief. In those days—the eighties of the last century—there was not a dining-room or restaurant in the works or anywhere near them where a young man accustomed to a decent standard of cleanliness could enjoy a meal. Sir Hugo has never forgotten the conditions under which he and his fellows then worked. " It has," he says, " never left my memory, and has contributed in no small way to humble but increasing efforts to give my workers what I was then without and what I missed most."

It may be mentioned here that there is perhaps no other firm in existence which excels the General Electric Company in the arrangements made for the comfort and well-being of the workers. The working conditions in the numerous factories, the heating, lighting, and ventilation are as perfect as care and forethought can make them. Dining halls and canteens have been instituted, where good food, perfectly cooked, is provided at a low price. Rooms are available for concerts, dances, and the like, and every facility is given for cricket, football, tennis, and all sorts of sports. The management is in every case left to the workers themselves.

In the course of his early work in London Sir Hugo came in contact with all sorts of people, inventors of all nations—Germans, Dutchmen, Belgians, Americans—and in conversing with these the young man's command of languages was extremely useful. This in turn brought him into touch with the head office, where the 'big strokes' of business were planned, and where there was more comfort and shorter hours than in the factory itself. He learned much about patent agents, patent laws, the financial interests of the City, and other useful matters—all of which were stored in his well-trained memory.

"My life was made up of curious mixtures," he says. "Sometimes I would be in the East End, existing on a few sandwiches, then in the afternoon I might be in the carriage of my managing director, taking distinguished foreigners through Hyde Park and to theatres in the evening; interesting, but leading to nowhere, so again I looked for the conscientious work to which I had been brought up.

"I had a position offered me with a Manchester firm. They wanted me to take over £10,000 worth of goods to Australia, and there to do business for them. Everything was packed up and all ready to go, and then the land crash happened in 1884. The time then was not suitable to start in Australia, and I refused to sail at the last minute. But I offered to work for an inconsiderable salary—as a sort of compensation to the firm—provided I was given a share in the profits in the scheme which

SIR HUGO HIRST 128

Photo Elliott & Fry, Ltd.

I suggested. This was that they should assist me to open a shop in London to sell the goods."

His firm agreed, and a shop was opened in Queen Victoria Street, where electric bells, medical coils, gas-igniters, and similar articles were sold. For the first two years there was very little money in it, but a great deal of hard work. Sir Hugo combined the duties of engineer, showman, salesman, and if he did not make much money gained a great deal of useful knowledge and experience. He made many friends in the engineering world, and realized more and more the possibilities of electricity.

He was particularly interested in electric light. At this date electric lighting was still in its infancy. The incandescent light was only about six years old, and people were slow to realize its value. A good many hotels and large business offices were being fitted with electric light, but very few private houses. Electric lighting was very costly, because each electric engineering firm made and installed all its own accessories, such as switches, lamp-holders, and dynamos. It was a most wasteful business, and Sir Hugo saw at once that the great need of the industry was a central organization to supply all these accessories.

With Sir Hugo, to form an idea was to act upon it, and he set to work without delay. He went to pottery-makers and got them to make china-base switches, he ransacked the glassware industry for shades, and induced the brass-founders to standardize brass galleries for lamp-shades. The industry was so undeveloped that in many cases he was actually obliged to invent the accessories required. News of the work he was doing came to the ears of the engineering firms, who bitterly resented it and put every obstacle in his way. He went on, regardless, and in 1887 produced a complete electrical catalogue, the first of its kind. This was the beginning of the General Electric Company, better known nowadays as the G.E.C.

The first works were at Chapel Street, Manchester, where a small factory was purchased and fitted up. Three to four hundred hands were employed, who made telephones, electric-bell indicators, cut-outs, wood-casing, and other articles. In 1900 the G.E.C. was registered with a capital of £85,000. At the time of writing the capital of the G.E.C. has increased to ten millions, and the profit is nearly a million yearly. It employs more than twenty thousand people, and has something like a thousand branches or agencies all over the world.

For some years progress was slow, but in 1893 public electrical supply-stations began to be built in Great Britain, and after that things moved more rapidly. In that same year, 1893, Sir Hugo started the Robertson Lamp Works at Witton, Manchester, and a little later purchased glass works at Lemington-on-Tyne to ensure a supply of bulbs. Then came a factory at Birmingham for electric-light fittings, and later works at Salford for the purpose of making instruments.

You may perhaps wonder at these factories being started in different parts of the country, instead of all being housed under one roof, for scattered factories might be thought to make for weakness. But the electrical industry is not like any other, for its needs are so various that the work must be done wherever the supply of raw material and suitable labour is available. In the case of the G.E.C. each factory is a living entity, and the men in charge have each a degree of freedom which is equal to that of the directors of an ordinary company. It is only natural that at times they make mistakes, but one of Sir Hugo's favourite sayings is: " A man who never makes mistakes never makes anything." Then, too, the mere fact that each head is ' on his own ' makes him proud of his factory. He wants it to be the best, and a spirit of healthy competition is good for all concerned.

The big difficulty of the early days of electric lighting was a suitable lamp for household use. Most of you who read this have also read of Mr Edison's early experiments in lamp-making—how he sent men all over the world to search for material best suited for the carbon filament, and how, after testing thousands of different materials, he found a species of bamboo which provided what was required. Even so the early lamps were very short-lived, and needed constant replacement.

But Edison's and Swan's patents for their carbon filament lamps gave them a monopoly, and it was not until 1893, when these patents expired, that other inventors could bring their inventions into the British and American markets. Somewhere about the same time that Sir Hugo Hirst started the shop in Queen Victoria Street Mr C. J. Robertson went to the Continent to experiment with new filaments, and after some years invented a new carbon filament far superior to anything yet produced. Instead of a natural fibre he used cottonwool dissolved in chloride of zinc into a sort of syrup. This syrup was squirted slowly through a small hole into a jar of alcohol, which process converted it into a fine, whitish thread, which, after drying, was quite tough. The thread was then baked and transformed into a hard and tough filament of pure carbon.

Returning to England in 1893, Mr Robertson took his

invention to Sir Hugo, who, in partnership with Mr J. Fraser, built the Robertson lamp-factory already mentioned, and installed Mr Robertson there as technical adviser.

Foreign-made lamps were pouring into Great Britain, and the new factory had to fight its way against heavy competition, but the Robertson filament gave its lamps a life so much longer than that of its competitors that it soon won its way to the top. It was, in fact, the best carbon lamp ever made, but even its inventor knew that there must be something better, and the G.E.C. were soon at work on experiments with metal filaments.

Lamps were made with a filament of fine platinum wire which gave a brilliant light, but failed, because within a very short time the intense heat melted the platinum. Then Professor Nernst invented a lamp with a tiny pencil of 'rare earths,' the same used nowadays in the incandescent gas-mantle. This, however, though it gave a good light, had disadvantages, and its brief promise did not divert inventors from a search for a suitable metal. Auer von Welsbach was the inventor who produced the first workable metal filament which he made of the rare metal osmium, but this again failed to become a practical commercial success.

Tantalum was the first metal to reach the commercial stage, but the inventors had already realized that another metal, tungsten, would make a far more efficient lamp. On the face of it the task of making a fine filament out of tungsten was a hopeless one. Tungsten ore is found with tin ore in Cornwall, Australia, and elsewhere, and pure tungsten is obtained in the form of a hard, heavy powder. Making 'ropes of sand' seemed to be just as easy as transforming this powder into a thin, tough filament. Yet in the end it was done, and the new filament gave *four times* the light of a carbon filament for the same amount of electrical energy.

But it was fragile—terribly so—and the breakages on the way from the factory to the user were appalling In spite of the wonderful economy of power the game seemed not worth the candle. Yet there was one man who whole-heartedly believed in the tungsten lamp. This was Sir Hugo Hirst, who proved his faith by ordering a *million* of them. The trade vowed that he must be mad, yet he sold the lot in a single season, and built the new Osram lamp works at Hammersmith, where a new method of manufacture was employed. The filament was made of drawn tungsten wire, which is so tough that it will withstand the constant vibration of a railway train, or even the shock of gunfire in a battleship.

For a time it seemed as if the perfect lamp had been found, yet this was not the case. The light given by an electric lamp depends on the temperature of the filament, and presently it was found that if an inert gas such as nitrogen was introduced into the bulb a higher temperature could be used without melting the filament. So came into being the gas-filled lamp, which—especially in the larger sizes—is quite twice as economical as the ordinary vacuum type of lamp. The gas used in these lamps is not nitrogen but argon, which was discovered by the genius of the late Lord Rayleigh. The modern type of electric lamp is fully six times as efficient as that which Robertson produced in 1893.

All the glass bulbs used in the G.E.C. factory at Hammersmith come from Lemington. Time out of mind the blowing of glass has been done by human breath, and while machinery superseded the human factor in nearly every other process of industry glass-blowing remained as it was. Then came the invention of the wonderful Westlake automatic bulb-blowing machine, and Sir Hugo had two of these installed at Lemington. 'Wonderful' is the only word to describe this really astonishing invention. Iron arms flash into a glass pot, pick up by suction exactly the right quantity of molten glass, and transfer it to blowpipes which work with an uncanny imitation of human skill and craftsmanship. Compressed air is supplied at the right moment, the glowing pear-shaped bubbles are formed with amazing speed and certainty, and each is automatically enclosed in a mould. In another instant the moulds fall apart in a cooling bath, and the bulbs travel in their hundreds along an endless chain to the annealing furnace. The Westlake machine took five years to complete, but driven by an electric motor is controlled by one man only, and saves an immense amount of labour.

In 1900 the G.E.C. established tube works at Witton and began the manufacture of lamp-carbon. These were the only works in the kingdom producing lamp-carbon, which is an absolute essential for various purposes of war. Sir Hugo knew this and knew that in case of a European war Great Britain would be in a bad way without this special material. The War Department refused to assist him, but fortunately the Admiralty authorities had longer sight. All through the years from 1900 to 1914 the G.E.C. continued its steady growth. Extensions at Witton, where the Company owns more than forty acres, were built for the production of electrical railway equipment, so that the Company was able to supply anything from one lamp for a pocket torch.

the size of a pea, up to a completely equipped power-station. In 1913 Sir Hugo, in conjunction with Pirelli and Company of Milan, laid down a large-scale electric cable factory at Southampton.

When the Great War broke out the value of Sir Hugo's foresight in being able to produce lamp-carbon became plain, and every factory of the Company was driven at feverish speed. The G.E.C. purchased Fraser and Chalmer's Works at Erith, where they were able to make the largest-sized steam-turbines, conveyors, and mining plant.

After the War the G.E.C. quickly turned back to peace works of various kinds, and Sir Hugo, realizing that progress depends on invention, built large research laboratories at Wembley. It is at Wembley that the Company has purchased a large piece of ground for playing-fields for its London employees, where a big sports meeting is held every summer.

One very interesting result of research by the G.E.C. is the wireless beacon. Hitherto it has been necessary to keep men stationed in lighthouses to tend the lamps. Lighthouse-keepers are the loneliest men in the world, and may be cut off from the mainland for months at a time by winter storms, but Trinity House anticipates the introduction of mechanical lighthouses, two of which are already in existence, one at the South Foreland and the other at Burnham in Somerset. At neither of these lighthouses are keepers stationed, for by the new G.E.C. system the lights are controlled from shore. Each lighthouse is fitted with a duplicate lamp, and if one breaks down the other comes into use. If both fail, an acetylene-burner is automatically lighted. These two lighthouses have worked so well that four others are to be changed over to a similar system, namely, the Pendeen, Lizard, Hartland, and Skerries. In addition, nearly a score of 'wireless-lighthouses' are being constructed. In these there is no light, but a hundred-mile-range beam is constantly sent out, by means of which vessels can always define their positions either by day or night, in sunshine or in fog. In these, too, the mechanism is duplicated to safeguard against breakdowns.

The rapid growth of wireless has caused the G.E.C. to build still another factory at Coventry, where the well-known Gecophone sets are made, and this factory also produces equipment for automatic telephones.

In 1925 Mr Hirst was made a baronet. He was already on the Advisory Council of the Board of Trade, the Committee of Unemployment Insurance, the Committee for Reorganizing the Marketing of Coal, and is now a member of the Industrial Council for the promotion of peace in industry. There is always peace in his industry, for there is a very happy spirit among all employees of the G.E.C., both small and great. Even the contributor was able to sense that during his brief visits.

You might think that a man like Sir Hugo, who is still active head of this enormous organization with more than a thousand branches, had time for nothing else but business. But this is far from being the case. He lives in the country, at Fox Hill, near Reading, and his hobby is experimental farming. He has there a wonderful herd of Jersey cows. He is President of the Reading Football Club, and if his own football days are over he still finds time to play both golf and billiards and occasionally to attend race-meetings.

Speaking of his own career, he says: "Success itself may not come rapidly, but boys should remember that experience of all kinds, wherever gained, is always valuable, and provides the sinews for the construction of the successful business man. In those days I learnt the rudiments of book-keeping, finance, accounts, the art of correspondence, and delegating duties to others, and how to make friends and to avoid the making of enemies. The lesson was taught me too that because a thing is interesting it need not, therefore, be a success. As I surrounded myself with personal friends I tried to inspire them with my ideals and to inculcate a spirit of *bonhomie* and of hard work, and make them feel that I was first servant rather than 'boss.' I shared long hours with them at work, and took part in all their recreations. My success at the latter led more to my eventual popularity than my more serious efforts!

"When building up my organization it has been my endeavour to study the psychology of the different people who were working with me. There are at the present day nearly a dozen men, who are my colleagues, who started with me originally in humble positions. I have tried to study the welfare of my workers outside their work, as well as during office hours, and have never lost sight of the human element in industry. I have always chosen my friends from among those men who have achieved something.

"When very young I chose the words 'I will' for my motto, and it remains the same to-day. My aim is constantly to advance and to consolidate. Hard work done intelligently is always repaid. Young people are apt to look at big organizations as institutions which have been there for ever; they should realize that everything has been started and built up by a man's striving and determination."

CHAPTER XII

"ALL HANDS MUST TURN TO!"

The Story of Lord Inchcape

"I BELIEVE I'm an older sailor than any of you," said Lord Inchcape, speaking to a roomful of distinguished sea-captains at the banquet of the Company of Master Mariners in 1927. "I went to sea no less than sixty-seven years ago, at a date before most of you present here to-night were born. I was just eight years old when I was taken for a voyage from Montrose to Archangel and back to Kirkcaldy in a barque of three hundred tons, called the *Asia*. She was just off the stocks. It took us a whole week to get through the Pentland Firth. Dead calm or head winds the whole time, and over and over again the tide carried us back and we had to cast anchor under Dunnet Head.

"At last the wind changed, and we got out into the Atlantic and reached the White Sea, and after four weeks' passage arrived at Archangel. During my stay there I picked up a few words of Russian which I still remember. But what I remember most clearly is the fact that twice I fell overboard in the River Dvina. The first time I was rescued by a Russian boy, the second by a ship's cook. If that cook had not caught me just as I was going down for the third and last time I should have missed a long and delightful life and the pleasure of being here to-night."

You notice that Lord Inchcape has enjoyed his life. That is interesting and instructive, because few men have worked harder than he. When he was already a man of seventy-five he said: "For forty years I worked on an average twelve to fourteen hours a day, and for the last ten years I have worked ten hours a day. Even on my holidays I have never worked less than three or four hours daily." If report can be believed the only time that Lord Inchcape did not work at full pitch was during his schooldays. Certainly at that time none of his friends ever dreamed that Jimmy Mackay would become the greatest shipping magnate in the country—one might say in the world—a millionaire, and a peer of the realm.

He came of a family which, as the saying goes, had the salt in its blood. His father was a sea-captain. He was born at Arbroath on September 11, 1852; at Arbroath and Elgin Academy he went to school; and in Arbroath began his business career. Speaking at that same banquet of the Master Mariners, he said: "At twenty-one I found my patrimony was a few sixty-fourths of a sailing-ship which brought me a modest income very much like what I have to-day. I don't know why you laugh. You must remember that freights were much higher in those days and the pay of skippers lower."

His father died when he was a boy of only ten, and as we have said he stayed on at Arbroath until he was about twenty. But like many young Scotsmen young Mackay was ambitious, and his thoughts were all of the East. The first step was to gain employment with an East India firm, and this he got with Mackinnon, Mackenzie, and Co., whose name was even then a household word throughout the East. After a short training in London he was selected to go to India as a junior; and in 1874 he sailed for Bombay. He very soon settled down to his new work, and, being blessed with a fine constitution, found himself able to stand the climate and to work as hard as he had been working in London. A young fellow who puts work first, and especially one who, like Mackay, has a canny Scottish head on his shoulders, is sure to get on; he rose fast, and it was not very long before he had gained a partnership. In a few years more he was head of the firm, and then turned all his great energies toward expanding the resources and trade of the British India Steam Navigation Company and the other interests of the firm.

While still a young man he was chairman of the Bengal Chamber of Commerce, Sheriff of Calcutta, a member of the Legislative Council of India, and on coming home in 1894 became a member of that very important body, the Council of India in London. For nearly half a century past his name has been even better known as a statesman than as a man of business. One of his earliest tasks was to serve on a Government committee for increasing the usefulness of the commercial intelligence service provided for manufacturers by the Board of Trade.

This sort of intelligence means everything to that part of the business world which is engaged in sending British goods to foreign countries. They require to know what countries want their goods, and exactly what sort of goods are wanted. Here are just two examples of the sort of thing. Before the War Lancashire was sending great quantities of turkey-red handkerchiefs to Russia, where women used them as head coverings. These handkerchiefs were oblong in shape, but the Russian preferred them square. The Germans found this out before the Lancashire cotton-manufacturers discovered it, with the result that the Germans flooded the market with cheap square handkerchiefs, and Lancashire lost the whole of this particular trade.

The second case was that of kitchen-knives for Servia. At one time Sheffield had the whole of this trade, but a German commercial traveller discovered that the Servian people liked a knife broader at the point of insertion in the handle than the English model. The German manufacturer at once yielded to the Servian whim, and made knives of the required shape. Their steel was nothing like so good as the British, yet for all that Germany stole the whole of the trade in this particular type of knife.

But in the East, owing to the good work of men like Lord Inchcape, British trade prospered. The three great export trades of Siam—rice, pepper, and teak—came into British hands. Rice was treated in English mills at Bangkok and shipped in British vessels. The clothing of the people of Burmah and Siam was made in England, and British machinery and hardware held the field to themselves. Fire and marine insurance were British monopolies, and the banks were all British and all shipments were financed by them.

The great success of Mr Mackay in Indian trade led to the Government's asking him to undertake the negotiation of the new Commercial Treaty with China, and in 1901 he went to China and spent a whole year in that country, with the result that the treaty was signed on September 5, 1902. That treaty is still the main basis of British trade with China.

We might easily fill this whole chapter with a record of the work done by Lord Inchcape, not for himself or his firm, but for the nation. He had, for instance, a great deal to do with the improvement of our Consular

Service. This service was at one time a disgrace to a great trading nation. More than half our Consuls were foreigners. They were ill-paid, slack, and casual, but there has been a great change for the better in the past twenty years.

Another task the Government asked him to undertake was an inquiry into Government workshops, where at one time there was a lot of waste and slackness. In 1906 he and the late Mr Huth Jackson and several others served on a committee to inquire as to whether it would be a good thing to have a sort of national insurance for ships in time of war. The work of this committee was tremendously important, for when the Great War broke out in 1914 a scheme of war-risk insurance was ready and was at once put into working.

He was at that time senior partner in a number of great business firms, a director of the Suez Canal Company, and a director of the British India Steam Navigation and other companies. On the British India (" B.I.") Company's fusion in 1914 with the P. and O. Company, Lord Inchcape became chairman of both. Two years later the P. and O. acquired a predominant interest in the Union Steam Ship Company of New Zealand, the New Zealand Shipping Company, and other shipping companies. From that time on the whole responsibility for this enormous business was on his shoulders. Some idea of the size and importance of the P. and O. and associated lines may be gained when we say that the number of passengers carried in 1927 was two and a quarter millions. The care with which this vast business is conducted will be gathered from the fact that this multitude of people was carried without the loss of a single life—and the record is not exceptional.

Lord Inchcape, needless to say, takes the keenest interest in the fortunes of the great P. and O. Company and its associated lines, as is proved by his speeches at the annual P. and O. meetings. At the meeting in 1926 he mentioned that there had been a protest against the fares charged on P. and O. ships to India. The first-class return fare to Bombay is £130. Lord Inchcape pointed out that the cost of living in a first-class hotel is at least £2 a day, and that no hotel supplies the luxuries of life provided in one of his liners. The double voyage takes forty-one days, so if you allow £2 a day for living expenses the travelling works out at only threehalfpence a mile, or the same as third-class fare on a British railway. The Company has to meet a colossal bill for upkeep and renewal of ships' furniture, plate, glass, linen, etc. Among other replacement items during the year 1927 were 92,977 wineglasses and tumblers and 276,787 cups, saucers, and plates, while the replacement of linen ran into a fabulous sum. "They tell me," said Lord Inchcape, "but I can't believe it, that at the end of a voyage pillow-slips are frequently utilized by ladies, when packing up, to make boot bags. I mentioned this the other day to a lady who frequently travels by these steamers, and the reply I got was, 'What an excellent idea! I never thought of it.'"

The carelessness of passengers adds enormously to the cost of carrying on a line of steamers, and Lord Inchcape once suggested that the following set of rules should be printed and posted in all the public rooms and cabins in his ships :

Do not leave tap on and plug in when leaving bathroom at night.

Insure baggage against all risks, and place valuables with the purser.

Use ash-trays and refrain from throwing cigar- and cigarette-ends on floor, couches, and tables.

Jerk fountain-pens on blotting-pads, not on the floor.

One of the biggest and most important pieces of work that Lord Inchcape handled in all his long career was the sale of Government and ex-enemy ships at the end of the Great War. During 1919 and 1920 he sold thirty-five million pounds' worth of Government standard ships and no fewer than four hundred and eighteen ex-enemy ships. In 1920, at the request of the Government, he went to India and sold the Mesopotamian flotilla of war-craft, realizing £1,080,000. The amazing part of all this was the cheapness with which he carried out these difficult tasks. The thirty-five million pounds' worth of standard ships were sold at an overhead cost of only £850! The four hundred odd ex-enemy ships which realized a little over twenty millions were sold at a cost of £30,000. Thereafter his disposal of ex-enemy and prize vessels continued up to the spring of 1927. Well might the salesman say, "I have earned a holiday." So he had; and he took a busman's holiday in one of the ships of his own line!

Speaking of this colossal task, the President of the Board of Trade said: "Lord Inchcape has been instrumental in selling this immense volume of tonnage without a single complaint of moment from any quarter. No one else could have done this."

Lord Inchcape's home is Glenapp Castle in Ayrshire, where he delights in entertaining his friends. Lord and Lady Reading, Lord Birkenhead, Sir John Simon, and many other well-known men and women are among his

LORD INCHCAPE
Photo L. N. A.

14

personal friends. But fond as he is of his beautiful home he is still first and foremost a sailor, and his real holidays are at sea. He owns a very fine steam yacht, the *Rover*, of 450 tons. On one occasion he rang up Lord Shaw of Dunfermline to tell him he was going across to Ireland to see his new P. and O. ship, the *Rawalpindi*, do her steam trials, and suggested that Lord Shaw should accompany him. Lord Shaw accepted, but when they were due to return it was blowing great guns. Most yachtsmen would have waited for the weather to moderate, but not Lord Inchcape. "The gale," says Lord Shaw, "seemed enough to shift Scotland, and I was thankful indeed when we got into Lough Ryan."

In writing of Lord Inchcape for youthful readers it is important to remember one aspect of his character He has always known how to play as well as how to work; and in the midst of his stupendous activities has been wise enough to break off for a few days' shooting, or a few days with the salmon-rod, or afloat. But it must not be supposed that his holidays are work-free. Wherever he may be a part of each day is set aside for attention, with his secretaries, to the contents of the dispatch box, which encloses the daily advices of his various partners and managers in London and elsewhere. Usually, as he himself has confessed, matters are so put before him that he has only to write a single word signifying assent, more rarely still to counsel 'no action.' This sounds easy, but is in fact the outcome of a lifelong contact with affairs, a rich experience, and the ability swiftly to seize the essentials of the problem of the moment. He has been a constant opponent of the principle 'all work and no play,' with the consequence that his friends have always known him as the reverse of 'a dull boy.' His speeches, whether on national affairs, the business of his companies, or, more rarely, on topics personal to himself, are always listened to with attention, and are spiced by the saving grace of a never-failing humour. His interest in sport is not for himself alone, but is extended to the young men and women of his business houses, so that, among those of other enlightened modern leaders of commerce, his firms' employees have time and opportunity afforded them for healthy recreations of various kinds. His ability to laugh at the right time was typified by an occasion when, clad in oilskins and a sou'wester, he made his way, in rough weather at the Nore, from one of his ships to another which was anchored near by, waiting for the tide. As the boat approached the anchored vessel the coxswain called for the accommodation ladder (*i.e.*, passenger staircase) to be lowered. The commander, mistaking Lord Inchcape for a pilot, shouted back from the bridge, "Isn't the Jacob's ladder good enough for you!" Up the Jacob's ladder Lord Inchcape went, climbed over the rail, and made his way to the bridge, where the skipper was soon joining in his chief's laughter at the mistake.

Among the thousands of officers, seamen, and others employed in the P. and O. and British India Companies' ships Lord Inchcape has many friends, from the commanders right down to the Indian serangs, many of whom have served the companies for a lifetime and are proud of a nod of recognition from the *burra sahib* on his frequent visits to their vessels.

When aboard his own ships Lord Inchcape often goes about and talks to members of the crew. One day he noticed a white-bearded serang and said to him, "You are surely an old man to be still at work."

The serang smiled. "*Sahib,*" he answered, "if you did not shave your beard it too would be white."

All his people are devoted to their chief, because, they say, he is never deaf to any well-founded complaint, and always ready to give good advice and smooth out any trouble. The result is that those who work for him are happy, and that strikes and troubles of that kind are almost unknown. All the best of the Labour leaders are his friends, especially Mr Havelock Wilson.

During the great strikes of 1926 Lord Inchcape did a deal of good work for his country, and after it was over made a call to the nation. "The coal strike," he said, "has cost the mine-worker seventy-three millions in wages, and the cost to industry has been five or six times as much. All hands must turn to with a will to repair the damage."

Lord Inchcape married in 1883, and had one son and four daughters. It was the third of these, the Hon. Elsie Mackay, who was lost in an attempted Atlantic flight early in 1928. Miss Mackay was herself a most experienced pilot. She had been taught to fly by Sir Alan Cobham and took her pilot's certificate in August 1922. She had her own plane, and, as Sir Alan said, a nerve of iron, and was a member of the Advisory Air Committee. She was a brilliant woman of many parts. Possessed of a highly cultivated artistic sense, she undertook in 1926 the decorating and furnishing of the eight new ships which the P. and O. Company had recently built, and the redecorating and renovating of the interiors of the earlier passenger steamers of the Company. Like her father she was an indefatigable worker, frequently putting in twelve or fourteen hours' work in a day. The suite in which Lord and Lady Reading returned from

India was decorated by her, and the ex-Viceroy declared that he had never travelled in greater comfort. All the world sympathized with Lord Inchcape in the loss of his brilliant daughter.

Lord Inchcape continues, as chairman and managing director, to care for the fortunes of the P. and O. and other enterprises, and is still a very busy man. One of the many institutions in which he takes an active interest is the Hydrographic Bureau, which has its headquarters in Monaco. No fewer than twenty maritime Powers have combined their services to unify the system of buoyage, sea-lighting, storm warnings, coastal and port signals, soundings, and the like. This work is of enormous value to the whole of the world's shipping, making navigation simpler and safer in all seas.

Lord Inchcape is also president of the International Shipping Federation, having been unanimously elected by representatives of the eight principal shipbuilding countries of Europe, and he is an honorary member of the Company of Master Mariners mentioned at the beginning of this chapter, to which he recently gave a donation of £5000.

Recognition by the Crown of his public services was not delayed. In 1892 he received the C.I.E., and in 1894 there was conferred upon him a Knighthood of the Indian Empire; in 1902, of the Order of St Michael and St George; in 1910, of the Order of the Star of India, of which order, in 1924, he was advanced to the rank of Knight Grand Commander. Meantime, in 1911, in recognition of many years' service on the Council of India, he was raised to the peerage, with the title of Baron Inchcape of Strathnaver, and on his return from India in 1924, after setting India's finances in order as chairman of the Indian Retrenchment Committee—a huge task, demanding statesmanship, infinite tact, and patience—he was created a viscount. In 1927 a rare honour was accorded him by his appointment as an honorary captain of the Royal Naval Reserve.

CHAPTER XIII

"NEVER DESPAIR—KEEP PUSHING ON"

The Story of Sir Thomas Lipton

ONE of the nicest things about Sir Thomas Lipton is that he is not the least little bit ashamed of his humble origin. In fact, he shows his good sense by being proud of it. "Any boy can rise if he will only stick to it," he often says, and all his life, both in work and play, he has stuck to his motto: "Never despair! Keep pushing on." A wonderful life his has been, and for that matter still is, for in spite of advancing years he still goes everywhere, talks to every one, and takes the liveliest interest in all that goes on.

Knowing that Sir Thomas was born in Glasgow, many people believe him to be a Scot. He is nothing of the sort, being purely Irish. Both his parents were Irish, but like so many of their country-folk they came to Scotland to better themselves, and it was just after they settled in Glasgow that Tommy was born. His father worked in a Glasgow cotton-mill, but his wages were small, and the size of his hungry family made it hard to keep them. At school Tommy heard stories of the streets of New York being paved with gold, and, having at last managed to find a chance to work his passage to America in the stokehold of a tramp-steamer, he set out, a lonely little adventurer of fifteen, across the Atlantic.

When the lad landed with a crowd of other immigrants

at Castle Garden, New York, it did not take him long to find the truth of the old Irish saying, "Far away cows wear fine horns." But he did not despair, and as he could land no other job took to selling newspapers around the Battery. But this was a temporary job, meant only to give him bread and butter until he got something better, and he kept his eyes and ears open for any offer that might come along. Some one told him that workers were wanted on the rice-plantations in South Carolina, and he went to the agency which was engaging hands, and was taken on. Of course he had not the faintest idea of what he was going to, and you can picture his dismay when, after nearly two days in the train, he landed up in a sort of dismal swamp. However, there was the work, and the pay, and the only thing was to buckle down. The heat was terrible, the climate shocking, and fever-laden mosquitoes swarmed both by day and night. Work went on for full six days each week, and the pay was so poor that it was almost impossible to save money. Tommy Lipton stuck it out for three years, until his health broke down entirely, and the plantation doctor told his employers that they had better discharge him if they did not want a corpse to bury. So at the age of eighteen the boy was back in New York, a living skeleton, with only a very few dollars in his pockets.

But if his body had suffered his mind had developed. He had learned a deal about men and matters during his hard apprenticeship in the Carolina swamps, and had made up his mind that the best road to success was working for himself instead of for others.

He used his small savings to return to Glasgow. The keen sea air did him good, and he was fairly fit and strong again when he arrived home after his three years' absence. He told his relations that he meant to start a shop, and asked them to lend him the money to do so. They were all poor folk, and surely it says something for the character and personality of this eighteen-year-old lad that he was able to persuade them to do so. But Tommy Lipton had, as he still has, an Irish tongue. At any rate, between them his friends put up a hundred pounds, and with this he took a little shop in Stobcross Street, Glasgow. It was a lock-up shop under tenement buildings, and he was very proud of it. He kept it spotlessly clean and made it as smart as possible. "There is a great deal in the appearance of a shop," he has said. "And perhaps still more in the treatment customers receive when they come in to make purchases." He called his shop "Lipton's Market," and sold groceries.

During his years in America young Lipton had come to realize the immense value of advertisement. At the period when he opened his first Glasgow shop, more than fifty years ago, shop-advertising was almost unknown in Britain. Big business, it is true, did a certain amount of sober advertisement, but the small shopkeeper did not dream of spending money in publicity. When he began business Tommy Lipton could not afford newspaper-advertisement. What he did was to get out a handbill which drew attention to his goods, and this he personally distributed to passers-by. Of course he worked single-handed, for he could not possibly afford any help. But very soon he turned his attention to newspaper-advertisement, and he plainly remembers that his first advertisement of this type cost him seven-and-sixpence, and described the merits of some specially fine bacon and ham which he had just purchased.

Then he got the idea of putting advertisements in his own shop-window, in the shape of striking or amusing cartoons referring to the goods sold within. One which proved very successful showed a very fat man and a very thin man riding together in the last compartment of a train. The stout traveller says to his companion, "Are you not afraid to travel in the collision compartment?" Whereupon the other answers with a smile, "Oh, no, not so long as I have a Lipton buffer opposite." Another showed an Irishman carrying a fat porker in a sack on his back. He meets a frock-coated, top-hatted gentleman who asks, "What's the matter with the pig, Pat?" To which Pat replies, "Sure, sorr, he's an orphan, so out of pity I'm taking him to Lipton." Bacon was always a specialty of the first Lipton shop, and a third cartoon showed a typical Irishman being towed down the street at a great pace by a very fine pig which he is trying to hold by a string attached to its leg. The title of the drawing is, "Lipton's Leading Article."

Another early advertisement resembled a Scottish one-pound note, and was inscribed "Great Irish ham, butter, and egg market. Ham, butter, and eggs given elsewhere for the value of one pound, given here for fifteen shillings." The date of this is March 1877. These notes were distributed broadcast throughout Scotland, and caused much talk all through the country. They also caused much trouble, for bank-managers frequently found them among bundles of genuine notes, and in the end Lipton thought it best to withdraw them voluntarily. The little shop became so well known and prospered so that its proprietor was able to pay back the money he had borrowed for the purpose of starting it, and to open a larger shop in the High Street, Glasgow, a much better neighbourhood.

"My two principles," he says, "were to make each transaction a cash one, and to cut out the middleman. In order to get rid of the middleman I had an agent in Ireland who bought butter, eggs, and bacon for me there. Once this agent nearly got me into trouble. He bought too freely for my limited resources, and when the bill came in I had not enough cash to settle it. Then it occurred to me that I possessed a good English silver watch. I took this across to a pawnbroker who lent me thirty shillings on it, just enough to provide the balance of the account and keep my engagement. It was not long, however, before I was able to redeem the watch."

By working hard, dealing honestly, and advertising freely young Lipton steadily built up his business, until in little more than a year he was able to hire assistants to stand behind the counters of his two shops, while he himself devoted his attention entirely to advertisement. He tried all sorts of what we nowadays call 'stunts.' For instance, he bought two of the finest, fattest white pigs he could find, had them carefully scraped and cleaned, tied pink ribands round their necks, and sent them waddling through the crowded streets, each led by a man dressed in pink, and having between them a third man carrying a banner, on which was inscribed the words, "We are going to Lipton's pink tea. Come along, yourself." They came—scores of them—so that the shop was crowded almost to suffocation, and business fairly roared.

So well known did Lipton become in Glasgow that he actually had a comic song devoted to his exploits. The ditty was dreadful doggerel, but it was sung in a music-hall by the popular comedian, J. C. Macdonald, and every street-boy in Glasgow soon knew it by heart. The chorus was this :

> Lipton's butter and ham,
> Lipton's butter and ham,
> That's the stuff to cram.
> Swallow his eggs, and they'll set ye on your legs,
> Tae ye're as auld as Methusalam.

When one shop succeeded Tommy Lipton promptly opened another. That sounds easy, but in practice it was nothing of the kind. Most young men, when they find success coming their way, begin to spend their earnings, to take things a bit more easily. But the more success Tommy Lipton gained the less he spent, and the harder he worked. His holidays were few and brief, and he kept on devising new schemes.

It would not be fair to say that he spent no money, for there was one object on which he never grudged spending—the comfort of his mother. He bought a house for her, and never let her want for anything. Irish families are known for their devotion one to another, and in Sir Thomas Lipton's handsome dining-room the first objects you will notice are two fine portraits on each side of the fireplace, one of his mother, the other of his father.

The young man had made his plan of life ; he was not content with any ordinary success, for he had the definite intention of becoming one of the world's great merchant princes. By long hours of toil, day in and day out, for years on end, he achieved his ambition. The first humble little shop in Glasgow grew to scores spread all over the country ; factories arose in many places, bearing his name and making the various products sold in his shops ;

tea-gardens were purchased in Ceylon, and fruit-gardens in England; Lipton's vans were on the high roads and Lipton's ships upon the sea, carrying cargoes of every sort of foodstuff. Ireland's supply of bacon was no longer sufficient to meet the demands of the ever-growing business, and it had to be supplemented by America's abundance. It may be news to some British readers that the Lipton pork-factory establishment in Chicago has killed as many as three thousand fat hogs in one day, and that Lipton's own many hundreds of freight-cars on American railways. Some idea of the vast growth of the business may be gathered from this fact—that the mere leaden lumps of the tea-chests, stripped off, produce a yearly revenue of something like £5000. Soon the firm was making its own soap, its own jam, and had its own tin-works, paper-works, and printing-works, and its head, while still a comparatively young man, had become a millionaire.

The rich man did not forget the days of his poverty, and in 1897, the year of Queen Victoria's Diamond Jubilee, he gave £25,000 for free dinners to the poor of London, and a little later, when the plague broke out in India, sent a cheque for a like sum to the relief committee. He also sent a large sum to the American Red Cross Society, to be used for the benefit of the soldiers wounded in the Spanish-American War. He is, and always has been, a staunch friend of America, and he has a pretty habit of causing the Union Jack and Stars and Stripes to float together over his establishments on big anniversaries. "I'm really half an American at heart," he has often said.

In 1898 Queen Victoria granted him a knighthood in recognition of his many charities, and in the same year his huge business was turned into a limited company.

One of the London evening papers had a poster that day, " The Great Lipton Scramble," meaning, of course, the scramble for shares in the new company. Another princely gift on the part of Sir Thomas was a cheque for the huge sum of £100,000 to establish the Alexandra Trust for the erection of cheap restaurants.

Having achieved fortune, Sir Thomas was able to turn his attention to his great hobby, yachting. Always he had been fond of games and sports of all kinds, and even during his hardest years he kept his health by open-air exercise. He began cycling when cycling was in its infancy, and he has played all games, from football to bowls and billiards. " When I see a boy who does not care for cricket or football," he says, " I conclude that there is something wrong with him. I have the feeling that he cannot be in good health." But the water has always been Sir Thomas's chief love. Brought up on the banks of the Clyde, he spent many an hour as a boy watching the passing craft and indulging in day-dreams of the boat he would buy if he could afford it. Whenever he had sixpence to spare he laid it out in boat-hire, and when, as was usually the case, his pocket was empty he would offer his services as rower or steersman, just for the pleasure of being on the water. But in all those early day-dreams he could hardly have foreseen the time when he would own the most famous racing-yachts in the world, a steam yacht the size of a small liner, and a fleet of auxiliary vessels.

It was pure chance that first put it into the mind of Sir Thomas to endeavour to win back the famous America Cup. The America Cup, a silver trophy of the original value of £100, was first offered for competition in the year 1851 to yachts of all nations by the Royal Yacht

Squadron, and was won on August 22 of that year by the American yacht *America* with the most consummate ease. With her sails set flat as boards she simply walked past all her numerous competitors.

What happened was this. In the spring of 1897 Sir Thomas was on his way from Paris to Rome and had with him in the same compartment the Hon. Charles Russell, who was on a diplomatic mission for the Canadian Government, while Sir Thomas was making for Naples *en route* for Ceylon. The two, both Irishmen, began to talk of yachting, and Mr. Russell spoke of the recent failure of another Irishman, Lord Dunraven, to recover the cup. "If one Irish boat has failed another might do better," remarked Sir Thomas. "Indeed, why should I not try it myself?"

Once he had formed the idea Sir Thomas was not long in making up his mind, and presently the challenge was issued on his behalf by the Ulster Yacht Club. Ulster, by the by, is Sir Thomas's own province, for his people came from County Monaghan. It was announced that the name of the new challenger would be *Shamrock*, and in a very short time the newspapers on both sides of the Atlantic were full of the story.

The Prince of Wales (afterward Edward VII) was as much interested as anyone, and proved it by paying a special visit to see the new yacht as soon as she was launched. *Columbia*, the property of the New York millionaire, Mr Pierpont Morgan, was selected to defend the Cup. She was built at a cost of £30,000, or about £5000 more than the price of the first *Shamrock*. *Columbia* had a novelty in the shape of a steel mast and boom. One thousand six hundred pounds was paid for her suit of sails, but those of *Shamrock* were even more costly, for they were woven to order of Egyptian cotton mixed with silk, and cost no less than 4*s*. a yard. Her great spinnaker of pure silk cost no less than 16*s*. per yard. Though *Shamrock I* was of only 135 tons measurement she carried no less than 14,000 square feet of canvas, whereas the original America had carried 6000 only.

The new yacht made a successful passage across the Atlantic under her own canvas, and the eyes of the whole world were on the race, or rather races (for there were three). But *Columbia* proved herself superior in the calm water and light winds of the American seaboard. She won the first two races outright, and in the third Sir Thomas's yacht met with an accident and was disabled.

Quite undiscouraged, the plucky Irishman had no sooner got home than he issued another challenge, and set to work to build a second *Shamrock*. She was built on the Clyde by Messrs Denny Brothers in absolute secrecy. The men employed on her worked at night, and during the day the shed was kept locked and guarded. Her frames were of nickel steel, and Sir Thomas spared no pains or expense to make her perfect. But she was never a success, and it is doubtful if she was as fast as her elder sister. The races were sailed in 1901, *Columbia* being again the defender and an easy winner.

Since each attempt to lift the Cup had cost Sir Thomas about £150,000 it might be imagined that he would have had enough. It is typical of the dogged resolution of the North Irish temper that he flatly refused to consider himself beaten, and announced his intention of trying again. *Shamrock III* was launched at Messrs Denny's yard in March 1903, and her first trials seemed to show that at last Sir Thomas had a winner. She was certainly very fast. Then a bad bit of ill-luck befell her. While out for a trial race against *Shamrock I* in Weymouth Bay the new yacht was caught in a sudden heavy squall. A screw in the main shrouds gave way, and the great steel mast snapped six feet above the deck. The steward, a man named Collier, was knocked overboard and drowned, Sir Thomas himself was pitched down the hatchway and badly bruised, and three members of the crew were injured. Sir Thomas immediately ordered a new mast and sails and declared the challenger would be off Sandy Hook at the appointed time in August. The firm of Ratsey and Lapthorn, who were commissioned to make the new mainsail, put on forty men and finished it in eight days, and *Shamrock III* was soon shipshape again.

The defender selected on this occasion was *Reliance*, a very beautiful craft belonging to Mr Oliver Iselin. *Reliance* was much lighter in construction than *Shamrock III*, and was handled by Captain Barr, who knew every twist and eddy of the tides. No one who had not spent years on the spot could hope to rival Barr's special knowledge of the course, and as usual light breezes and a calm sea were in his and *Reliance's* favour. *Shamrock III* put up a splendid fight, but in the end was defeated.

This third effort cost Sir Thomas, so it is said, £200,000, yet even so he did not give up hope of eventually recovering the much-coveted trophy. But pressure of business prevented a fresh effort for some years, and it was not until 1913 that he issued a fresh challenge and built his fourth *Shamrock*. This vessel, designed by Mr Nicholson, was simply a racing-machine, but a very beautiful one. She had no cabin, and her interior was merely a hollow shell covered in by the deck. She was built of cedar and sycamore, with an outer casing of mahogany. For crossing the Atlantic the only furniture was cots for

SIR THOMAS LIPTON 160
Photo Vandyk

the crew and officers and a stove for cooking. In her trials *Shamrock IV* beat *Shamrock III* with ease, and Sir Thomas, as well as every one else, had high hopes of at last proving that a British yacht could cross the Atlantic and beat the Americans in their own water.

It was not to be. *Resolute*, the American defender, was too fast and too tricky for the sturdier British yacht, and once more Sir Thomas had to acknowledge defeat. Even then, had it not been for the Great War, there is no doubt but that Sir Thomas would have tried again. But the War left Britain a comparatively poor nation, and incidentally doubled the cost of shipbuilding, and now that matters are becoming more normal Sir Thomas is hardly young enough to withstand the tremendous strain of such a contest, for he was born in the year 1850.

Apart from the lifting of the Cup Sir Thomas has realized most of the dreams of his youth. He played the nursery game of 'pretending,' and found all pretences true. Like most boys he dreamed of soldiering as he watched the Highland Light Infantry march lightly up a Glasgow street. Years later he proudly rode up that very street at the head of that battalion, as its honorary colonel. He dreamed of being friends with great men, but he could hardly have looked forward to the day when he would be a personal friend of the most popular monarch in the world, Edward VII. He dreamed of a yacht, and has owned a greater number of racing-yachts than any living man. He may have dreamed of titles—he has never said so—but now he is a baronet, a Knight Commander of the Victorian Order, a Grand Officer of the Crown of Italy, and one of his Majesty's Lieutenants of the City of London.

He thinks little of titles, and vows that his own rewards

have been far above his just deserts. "If," he says, "we would only make the practice of rewarding with our appreciation the achievements of each individual personally, instead of worshipping a man for the achievements of his fathers, we should have a much better country to live in than we actually have to-day."

Perhaps his best reward is the popularity which he enjoys. He is never Sir Thomas to his friends, but just Tommy Lipton. He is equally popular with the people in his employ, and his various businesses have been wonderfully free from strikes or troubles of that kind.

Apart from yachting his principal amusements are music and gardening. "Singing and playing," he says, "are among the real recreations of life, especially in bad weather and when you are not in the mood for books." He has played the violin, "in his own fashion," since he was ten years old. As for gardening, this, he thinks, the most perfect of recreations. It gives you, he says, just enough to think of to be a complete distraction, yet not enough to worry you. He has always been an early riser, and even in his busiest days would try to get an hour in his garden before going off to the office. All his life he has managed comfortably with only seven hours' sleep. He hates gambling. Thousands of pounds have been wagered on the Cup races, but he never put a pound on in the shape of a bet. He has never made a bet in his life.

He is fond of boys, and declares that it would be an excellent thing for English boys to be sent to America at the age of seventeen for a couple of years. The best sort of apprenticeship, he calls it, and vows that his own years in America helped him more than anything else to the position he has since occupied.

CHAPTER XIV

SELLING MEALS TO GREAT BRITAIN

The Story of Sir Joseph Lyons

NEVER be afraid of making false starts, but if you do make a bad one go back to the beginning and start all over again." That advice which he often gave to others was one of the secrets of the success of the late Sir Joseph Lyons. And another saying of his, one which he always lived up to, was, " There is no fun like work."

Like so many successful men, Sir Joseph Lyons started life quite humbly. His home was in Kensington, which is not one of the prettiest or most prosperous parts of London, and which in his early days was a good deal less prosperous than it is now. He had just the average education that a poor boy got in those days, but he had one thing which is not common to all boys. That was a great love for beauty and beautiful things. This was part of his nature. Another part of his make-up was a firm intention to get on.

He began his career as apprentice to an optician, a man who makes spectacles, and he himself invented a new sort of stereoscope. But he did not see a fortune in this or in spectacles. So, making up his mind that this was a false start, he turned artist. He worked in water-colours, and became quite a good painter. Some of his pictures were exhibited at the Royal Institute, and quite a number were sold. Many well-known people bought his pretty sketches, among them Sir Spencer Wills and Admiral Sir E. Wilmot. "Joey" Lyons, as he always liked to be called, worked very hard at his pictures, but, like all real artists, he hated selling them. "When I had done something that pleased me," he said, "something I had taken a delight in making, it seemed an outrage to exchange it for money." At last he made up his mind that he would make his living in some other way and paint for his own pleasure.

Artists are supposed to be the worst of business men, and certainly many excellent painters live poor and die poor, because they have not a notion how to sell their pictures. Others who do sell their work let the money slip through their fingers, and never have a pound with which to bless themselves. For an artist to turn himself into a business man is almost unheard of, and there was the added objection that by this time Joey Lyons was more than thirty years old, an age at which it is not too easy to make a fresh start in life.

His chance came quite suddenly, and here is the story of how it came. Mr Montague Gluckstein, partner in the old-established firm of cigar-makers, Salmon and Gluckstein, was anxious to start a catering business. Montague Gluckstein was then acting as traveller for his firm. A traveller, if he is to be any use at his job, must keep his eyes open to what the public wants, and Mr Gluckstein had long realized that there was nothing the public wanted more than good, cheap restaurants.

The catering of those days—forty years ago—was simply dreadful. Of course there were good restaurants, but they were expensive—far beyond the purse of the ordinary man in the street. Besides there were not

SIR JOSEPH LYONS
Photo Topical

many of them. The ordinary man visiting a strange town and wanting a meal had a choice between a public-house, where he would get cold meat, pickles, and beer, or a coffee-house, with its dirty little horse-box-like compartments, untidy shirt-sleeved waiters, grimy table-cloths, bad food, and worse smells. The tea-shop, such as we have everywhere to-day, was simply unknown. In those days every man who could possibly manage it went home to his own house for his midday meal, and most of those whose places of business were at a distance from their homes took sandwiches to the office and ate them there.

Montague Gluckstein was one of those who had suffered for years under this state of things. Sometimes he had nearly starved, and sometimes suffered severely from indigestion. He made up his mind that there was money in good, cheap restaurants, and he took the idea home to his brothers and laid it before them. He had even made out a rough budget of such an undertaking. Then, to use an Americanism, he 'struck a snag'—a very unexpected snag, for his brothers did not like the idea at all. To put it briefly, they thought it was beneath the dignity of an old-established cigar firm to launch out into the catering trade. Such a prejudice seems laughable in these days, but it was very real in the times of Queen Victoria.

Montague Gluckstein stuck to his guns, and in the end came to terms with his family. They would put up the money on condition that the family name was not used in connexion with the new undertaking. He must find some one to act as deputy whose name could be used. It is quite certain that not one of them—not even Montague himself—had the faintest notion that they were starting a business which would, within a lifetime, employ 30,000 people and have a capital of £8,000,000.

The next thing was to find the right man, and Montague at once thought of Joseph Lyons. Joe was a second cousin of the Glucksteins, and Montague, knowing he was smart, clever, and of good appearance, posted off to see him. He found him at Liverpool, where he was running a stall at an exhibition, and the two had a talk. Joe was quite ready to lend his name and to tackle the business. In fact, the suggestion appealed to him very strongly, for he too had suffered from the bad restaurants of the time, and he was full of ideas on the subject of pretty tea-rooms, with clean linen, bright new paint, and nicely dressed waitresses. In a very few hours the whole business was settled, an agreement was written out on an ordinary half-sheet of notepaper and signed, and it was agreed that a start should be made by securing the catering rights at the Jubilee Exhibition, which was shortly to open at Newcastle.

Joe Lyons plunged into the new venture with all his energy. He could talk and organize as well as paint, and as soon as he had secured the catering rights at Newcastle he put up a very smart kiosk and started serving the best tea at twopence a pot, instead of threepence a cup which was the regular charge at that time. The place was well ventilated and lighted, it was kept beautifully clean, the tables were covered with white cloths, with a vase of fresh flowers on each, and the waitresses were nice-looking girls, neatly and smartly dressed. The place was a success from the very first, so much so that when the exhibition threatened to close prematurely it was decided to keep the kiosk going as a tea-shop.

Another novelty was music every afternoon and evening, and this proved a tremendous attraction.

Keepers of old-fashioned restaurants shook their heads, vowing that it was all nonsense. "Lyons can't pay an orchestra out of twopenny cups of tea," they vowed. "We have only to sit tight and watch him go bankrupt."

The new firm did not go bankrupt, and the elderly 'fossils' got the shock of their lives when they heard that Lyons had engaged a famous Hungarian band with Barcza as leader. "Barcza," said Sir Joseph years afterward, "was a fierce-looking little man with an ugly, pock-marked face. But, my goodness, how he could play the violin!" The cost of this orchestra was no less than £150 a week, and again every one wondered how on earth Lyons could afford such an extravagance. Yet he did make it pay—out of tea, cake, and bread and butter—and at the end of the exhibition even the brothers of Mr Gluckstein, who had at first thrown cold water on the venture, were satisfied that they were on a good thing, although they certainly did not realize that the foundation had been laid of what was to prove the greatest catering system in the world.

Because the Newcastle venture had paid so well it was decided to bid for the catering at the Glasgow Exhibition. This was the biggest exhibition held in any part of the Empire since the London Exhibition of 1862. It covered sixteen acres, and was visited by Queen Victoria and nearly six millions of her subjects. The contract was secured, and the firm took the Bishop's Palace Tea Rooms, which were redecorated and thoroughly brought up to date. Lyons had a new sensation in store for the visitors, who found themselves waited on by scores of pretty girls all dressed alike and wearing Marie

Stuart caps. The cost of these costumes was heavy, but the result was a splendid advertisement, and the girls were kept busy all day long.

The weather that summer was wonderfully fine, and the attendance far larger than had been anticipated, so that often Joey and his partner had their work cut out to handle the crowds and feed them. However, all went well until the very last day, when there was such a rush that before the lunch-hour was over the last scraps of food were disappearing down hungry throats, and the manager sent an S.O.S. to his chief.

Remember there were no motors at that date, and it was not as easy to rush up fresh supplies as it is now. But Joe was not dismayed. He chartered every vehicle he could find, horse-cabs, horse-vans, even hand-carts, and sent messengers hurrying to every provision shop in the city. Within less than an hour more than twenty tons of food had been collected as well as large quantities of drinkables, and before the Exhibition closed that night more than fifty thousand people had been fed. It was at Glasgow that Joe Lyons first met that amazing man, Sir Thomas, better known as "Tommy," Lipton, and became very friendly with him.

"Lyons' widows," as people called the girls in their Marie Stuart caps, were such a success that when the great Paris Exhibition opened in 1889, and Messrs Lyons and Co. took on the "All British" restaurant, the girls went too. A whole shipload, most of them Scottish lassies who had never before been out of their country. Some of them did not like Paris and hurried home, but these were soon replaced, and once more the new firm registered a big success.

Now at last came the time to start in London, and

Lyons and Co. took over the catering at Olympia. The contract was made with Barnum and Bailey, who were showing there at the time. Another circus was in London that summer, at Covent Garden, and the latter had a poster on all the hoardings showing a wild horse of Tartary carrying a lion on its back.

George R. Sims chaffingly asked Barnum if he was going to let the other man beat him at advertisement, to which the latter replied, "I guess not. I am going to arrange for my refreshment caterer to ride round the ring and shall advertise him as 'Lyons on horse-back.'"

After this Lyons and Co. catered for the Crystal Palace, then started the series of tea-shops which all Londoners know so well. The first of these was opened at 213 Piccadilly in the year 1894, and was successful from the very beginning, and after that they spread so fast that soon they could be found all the way from Kensington to Aldgate.

The great point about these shops was that the prices were the same whether in the east or west. This was one of the secrets of their great success. "The public," said Mr Lyons, "likes a restaurant where they know they can get a certain article at a certain price; it saves them the trouble of thinking. It doesn't occur to them that the rent in Piccadilly is higher than the rent in Aldgate, but in spite of that it would never do to raise our prices in the West End. If we did, and people found that they had to pay an extra penny for a cup of tea in Piccadilly, why then they would think twice before they went into another depot." What scientists call 'psychology' goes for a lot in business, but it only means getting into the mind of the people who are likely to be your customers, realizing what they want, and acting accordingly. This is one more of the secrets of success.

To-day the slogan of Lyons is, " No gratuities," but at the period of which we are writing the old system of tipping was still in force. It had always been the custom in the catering trade to allow the public to pay the wages of the waiters, and it had not occurred to the managers of the new firm to make any alteration. But Lyons was the first firm to employ women waitresses on a large scale, and it was soon clear that the tipping system must go. Letters appeared in the newspapers on the subject, and there were jokes in the comic papers about " The Lyons and the Lambs." Mr Gluckstein and Mr Lyons consulted, and the result was a new system of payment for all waitresses, which made them independent of tips, and notices in all the tea-shops and restaurants, " As from to-night—no gratuities."

The firm was expanding fast, and so many well-dressed and comparatively wealthy customers used the tea-shops that Mr Lyons put it to his partners that it would be a good plan to start better-class catering to be run on similar lines. " Good quality, cheap prices, no tips." The partners did not see anything against it, so Lyons started the big Trocadero just off Piccadilly Circus, the Throgmorton in the City, the Popular Café in Piccadilly, the Blenheim in Bond Street, the first Corner House, and a lot more, and very soon they were all going as strongly as the older tea-shops.

The old Trocadero occupied barely half its present site, and was entirely reconstructed by its new owners. This work proved far more expensive than had been anticipated and cost the enormous sum of £100,000. All the money was found by the firm.

One of the best advertisements Lyons ever got was from the late King Edward. "I like Mr Lyons," he said. "He feeds my people well." And a great statesman, now passed away, said of him, "Mr Lyons is the greatest temperance reformer in the country." This was quite true, for the attractive tea-shop tempts many people who used formerly to feed in public-houses.

Before long Lyons began to reach out for fresh worlds to conquer. The firm had more tea-shops and restaurants than could easily be counted, so started a tea business. They became wholesale tea-merchants, and soon had thousands of agents selling their teas all over the country.

You will remember how Mr Lyons had said to himself that once he had made enough money he would go back to painting. He never did so, but the odd thing is that he took to another branch of art—that of writing stories. He wrote a couple of novels in collaboration with Cecil Raleigh, then turned his pen to detective-stories, and very good they were too. In one of them the murderer completely disappears, and Scotland Yard is entirely baffled, for they cannot imagine where the man has gone. In the end it is found that the murderer has enlisted in the Police Force.

It is hardly likely that the author knew of it, but this very thing actually happened in Scotland. A young Perthshire gillie had a row with a big blackguard which ended in a fight. The Perthshire boy, who was a bonny fighter, hit the other so hard that he killed him. That same evening he went off across the hills, and after walking all night reached Dundee, where he enlisted under another name in the police. There he did good work for many years, and there were very few folk who knew that the stalwart bobby was the same man who killed the bully with one blow of his fist.

Mr—we should now say Sir—Joseph Lyons had other interests besides his business and his play. He had already joined the Territorial Army, and was the first to introduce athletics into the Territorial plan. He organized the first Territorial Athletic meeting which was held at Stamford Bridge in June 1909, and which attracted 1700 entries. The prizes were presented by the Duchess of Fife. The meeting was so successful that a great national organization was formed, and in 1910 the Territorial Sports took place at the Crystal Palace and had entries from all over the country.

Sir Joseph's well-earned knighthood brought him congratulations from all over the country. Letters came from Lord Esher, Lord Burnham, Lord Northcliffe, the Chief Rabbi, many actors, and many Territorial officers. But what he valued more than any others were letters from less well-known folk whom he had befriended. For, like all really big men, Sir Joseph was immensely charitable. He never talked about his charities, but he helped many and did it wisely. One of the charities in which he was most interested was the Little Sisters of the Poor, and no one need be told what wonderful work these kind women do. Many stories are told illustrating the kindness of Sir Joseph's heart. Here is one. On a Saturday night two young Oxford 'undergrads' who had been dining at the Trocadero said to him that they were not sleepy and would like to know of a supper club where they could have a good time for a couple of hours. Sir Joseph appeared to consider the matter, then he spoke. "Do you want to have a really good time," he asked, "the time of your life?"

" Rather ! " said both at once.

" All right, but it will cost you something—a couple of pounds apiece. If you are game for that amount I will put in the same."

The youngsters looked rather puzzled, but agreed to share in the adventure. They were still more puzzled when Sir Joseph went to the cashier and changed the money into half-crowns. The three sallied out into a chilly autumn night, and Sir Joseph led the way down to the Embankment, where the homeless and destitute were sleeping on the seats.

Beginning at Westminster they walked down the Embankment, rousing the sleepers, hearing their stories, and distributing their silver. The students entered into the spirit of the thing most thoroughly, and in the end gave away double their original two pounds. At the end they said to their guide, " Well, you know what's what. We never enjoyed anything so much in all our lives."

Sir Joseph had a keen eye for trouble of any sort. One day a good many years ago he was walking quietly down Piccadilly, smoking and thinking over some new scheme, when he began to have an idea that he was being followed. Looking round, he saw a small and rather ragged boy following. He crossed the street, but still the boy followed, watching him all the time.

At last Sir Joseph stopped and turned. Before he could speak the boy began. " Ain't you done with it yet, guv'nor ? " he asked sharply. " You'll be burning your moustache if you smokes it much longer."

" What do you mean, my boy ? " asked Sir Joseph.

" It's Dad," said the boy. " He's a cripple at home. He can't afford no tobacco, but he do love a smoke, and I been follering you, waiting for you to chuck away your cigar." Sir Joseph questioned the boy, who was only nine years old, and you may be sure that crippled father of his was able to enjoy a real smoke for a long time to come.

Story-writing, painting, Territorials, charities, the theatre—he rarely missed a play—you might well suppose that Sir Joseph Lyons in his later years must have left the business to his competent managers. But he did not. He was in conference with his partners almost every day, and although, even before his death, his firm was feeding more than three-quarters of a million people daily the detailed accounts of his three hundred branches were passed at headquarters the very next morning, and takings and profit analysed to a penny.

One of the biggest losses in the restaurant business comes from breakages, and Sir Joseph was one of the first restaurant owners to go into this matter from a sensible point of view and see how the loss, which amounted to thousands a year, could be cut down. He found that certain people have a 'special susceptibility' to breakages—in other words, they are natural, born smashers, and cannot be cured. They may, however, be quite good workers, so that the best thing is to put them on a job where they are not dealing with cups and saucers. By this and other sensible suggestions he cut down the breakages bill quite considerably. The principal secrets of the great success of the Lyons business are the care with which the buying is done and the system by which waste is eliminated. "It seems like a fairy-tale," said Sir Joseph to an interviewer, "but it is true that if in the Trocadero six stalks of asparagus were stolen in the course of the day the theft would be discovered next morning."

The whole vast machine goes with the punctuality and

regularity of a fine watch. To give just one example of the extraordinary care taken over details. Every order received in the kitchen is stamped the exact minute at which it arrives, and a similar stamp tells the exact minute at which the dish is dispatched to the dining-room.

Sir Joseph lived through the worst of the War and did rather more than his bit in helping to feed the nation at a time when food was desperately scarce.

The firm of Lyons continues to grow and to-day employs 30,000 people. Its headquarters at Cadby Hall, Kensington, cover eleven acres, and at Greenford it has a great factory thirty acres in extent which deals with tea, cocoa, coffee, chocolates, and confectionery. At their various shops and restaurants Lyons and Co. serve ten million meals a week, and the list of good things which their customers devour is amazing.

Think of two million portions of ice-cream daily! Does it not make your mouth water? In a week their factories turn out two and a quarter million rolls, 500,000 Swiss rolls, 125,000 cakes, a quarter of a million cream and jam sandwiches, and three-quarters of a million muffins and crumpets.

There is perhaps no other firm in the country which takes more interest in their employees than that of Lyons. If you look at the firm's pay-list you see in it the names of doctors, dentists, chiropodists, even manicurists, whose services are at the command of the staff of Lyons.

There are also large numbers of musicians. You may hardly believe it, yet it is a fact that no less than £150,000 a year is paid in salaries and expenses to the various orchestras employed by the firm.

A magnificent sports club has been formed at Sudbury for the benefit of Lyons' workers. Here are seventy acres of fine grounds with opportunities for every sort of game, from football to croquet. Another interesting thing which the firm has done is to start schools for waitresses. There is one at St John's Square, Clerkenwell, and another at the Corner House, Piccadilly.

The whole growth of Lyons has been natural. Because the bread served in the tea-shops was good, customers asked to be allowed to buy it, and so the great bakeries came into existence, which now sell 130,000 loaves and half a million rolls daily.

Because the ices were good and cheap their output has risen to two million portions daily. And the growth goes on. Give the public what they like, and they will come for more. There is the secret.

SIR CHARLES MACARA

Photo Elliott & Fry, Ltd.

CHAPTER XV

THE MAN WHO WORKED FOR OTHERS

Sir Charles Macara's Great Career

THE story of Charles Macara really begins in the year 1862, when a tall boy of sixteen arrived in Manchester to take a berth with a firm of cotton merchants in Mosley Street, but we are going to jump no less than twenty-four years and start on a stormy evening in December 1886, when Mr Charles Macara, whose name was already known throughout Lancashire as one of her greatest business-men, was standing on the beach at St Annes-on-Sea, watching for the return of the lifeboat which had gone out to the rescue of a vessel which had been sending up rockets out in the blackness off-shore. Mr Macara was very keen about lifeboat-work, and as he was personally acquainted with all the men in the crew he found it anxious work peering out into the gloom of the driving storm. At last came a shout, "There they are!" and the boat was seen flung high on the top of a great wave. It vanished in the trough, rose again, and came driving safely on to the beach, to be hauled up by dozens of willing hands. Five soaked and exhausted men were landed, who had been rescued from the mast of a small vessel wrecked on Salter's Bank.

It so happened that on this very evening a concert was being held in the town for the lifeboat fund, and after being fed and dressed in dry clothes the five rescued men were brought by Mr Macara to the hall where their Scottish skipper told in simple words of how he had been saved.

A week or two later a fearful storm blew up, and the steamship *Mexico* of Hamburg, bound for Liverpool, was driven on the terrible sandbank between Southport and Formby. Three lifeboats, those of Southport, Lytham, and St Annes, put out, and there was little sleep that night in the three towns, for the storm raged more and more furiously. At dawn the Lytham boat returned with the wrecked crew of the German vessel. Both the other boats had been capsized in the raging sea. Of the fifteen men in the Southport boat two only escaped with their lives, while of the thirteen who manned the St Annes boat all were drowned. One by one the bodies were flung up by the waves, and reverently laid in the churchyards.

At that time the Lifeboat Institution had been in existence for more than sixty years, but it had no funds to meet such a disaster as this. Mr Macara flung himself into the business of raising a relief-fund, for the widows and orphans. He was made chairman of the fund, and in little more than a fortnight no less than £33,000 had been gathered. Hamburg sent £1400, but the rest of the money was raised in this country. Mr Macara found that it had been the custom of the Institution to offer the widow and family of a lifeboatman who had lost his life in attempting to save those of others a grant of £100. This was a poor recompense for the loss of the bread-winner. Going into the matter, Mr Macara found that this was all that the Institution could afford, for its whole income was only £42,000 a year, and only 25,000 persons out of all the millions in this country were contributing. Seeing that lifeboats had already saved 35,000 lives, this was clearly absurd, and he decided to make an appeal through the Press. He boldly asked for £100,000 a year.

Since inland cities knew nothing of lifeboat work he brought the lifeboats and men from Southport and St Annes to Manchester, and organized a great procession. The boats were launched on the lake in Bellevue Gardens, and an exhibition was given of life-saving. The result was splendid. Manchester's contribution jumped from £200 to £4000 a year, and Lancashire and Yorkshire together contributed £21,000, instead of £8000 as formerly.

Liverpool, Glasgow, and Dewsbury held lifeboat processions, while Sheffield had one which was no less than three miles long, with Grace Darling and her father impersonated in one boat. Lifeboat Saturday in Birmingham drew a crowd of 40,000 people. The income of the Lifeboat Institution rose from £42,000 in 1891 to £137,000 in 1919. Small wonder that the Institution was grateful, and that it put its gratitude on record. In the issue of its journal for August 1, 1894, appeared the following:

> We cannot but specially mention Mr and Mrs Macara, both of whom have thrown themselves heart and soul into the work, and have done wonders in developing the Lifeboat Saturday.

Reading all this, you may ask what it has to do with the story of a great business man. The answer is that it illustrates the character of the subject of this chapter as no amount of description can do. In his *Recollections* Sir Charles says: " An invaluable quality I got from my early days was the consciousness of the claims of the other side ; in other words, the Christian teaching 'Do unto others as ye would they should do unto you' took, I hope, good root in my character." This is the keynote of his career, for all through a very long life he has tried to be fair to both sides. If a strike were on he could always see and understand the strikers' point of view, and that is the reason why there is no employer in the cotton trade better liked by men as well as masters.

Another point which this lifeboat story brings up is this—that, however busy a man may be in trade or commerce, he can always find or make time to help others. But we must get on with our story.

Charles Macara was the eldest son of a Scottish minister, the Rev. William Macara, a man of great heart and will, yet always thoughtful and considerate to others. Charles was the eldest of seven children, and was born at Strathmiglo in Fifeshire in 1845. His mother was an equally fine character, and although the family were by no means well off young Charles had as good a home as any boy could wish for. His mother, left an orphan at five, had been brought up by an uncle who had risen from a very humble position in the Indian Civil Service to be Chairman of the great East India Company, and naturally Charles as a boy heard much of the exploits of his great-uncle. "No words," he says, "can paint how great a hero he was to my youthful imagination." It was his great-uncle's exploits as a soldier that made the greatest appeal to Charles's mind, and his chief ambition was to enter the army and go to India.

It was not to be. Instead he went, as we have seen, to Manchester and became a clerk in a firm of cotton merchants. He had cheap lodgings in Rusholme, and spent his days poring over ledgers and examining patterns of cotton cloth by the rather faint light which filtered through panes of frosted glass. One of his chief memories of that time is " the sweet, exotic smell of raw calico which gives Manchester its characteristic plantation smell, the smell of Uncle Tom's Cabin." He had very little money and, of course, few amusements, but if he was not born with a silver spoon in his mouth he had inherited qualities which were of much more value than wealth. One was splendid health and an iron constitution, another a power for hard work and a desire to get on, a third was that desire to be fair to others, which has been the keynote of his great success in life.

He got on ; he was bound to get on. The complaint that the authors of this book have to make against the great men whose stories they are trying to tell is the difficulty they have had in getting their heroes to explain just how it was that they did get on. The fact is that, to men with such qualities as they nothing else seems possible but success, and most of them are far more interested in telling of matters outside their actual business than in describing how they made the groundwork of their fortunes.

One thing is certain, Sir Charles got on very fast, for while he was still in his twenties he was made Manchester representative of one of the greatest of Scottish cotton firms, and by the time he was thirty-six he was managing partner of an old and well-known firm and already able to take part in the public life of this great city.

Cotton, the trade in which Sir Charles has always been engaged, is one of the world's greatest industries, for cotton forms nine-tenths of the clothing of its population. The odd thing is that England, which does not and cannot produce an ounce of cotton, is the greatest cotton-manufacturing country. Lancashire buys and brings three thousand miles across the Atlantic one-fifth of the American cotton-crop ; she buys and brings from Egypt one-half of the Egyptian crop ; she spins, weaves, dyes, and prints it ; and, after keeping about one-quarter of the made cloth for the home market, exports the rest to every corner of the earth. India and Japan are her chief customers, but all countries take English cotton goods, and in spite of a 60 per cent. tariff some of it actually finds its way back into the United States.

The firm of Charles Bannerman and Sons, which Sir Charles Macara has managed for nearly half a century, has always been in the front of the trade and of the trade's battles for British supremacy.

It has not been all plain sailing. Fifty years ago the cotton-trade of Manchester was stationary. It was not going ahead at all. As Sir Charles says, there were signs of senile decay. It was quite clear that something must be done to buck things up, and that something came into being as a project for a great ship canal, so that Manchester might bring her cotton straight to her own docks, instead of bringing it by rail from Liverpool. On June 27, 1882, a meeting was held in a certain drawing-room in Manchester, at which grave-faced business men, Mr Macara among them, discussed the possibility of such a canal; on January 10, 1894, the canal was opened, and seventeen days later the first cargo of cotton sailed direct from America into Manchester.

Will you believe it, there were spinners in Manchester who refused to take advantage of the canal and who still had their cotton sent to Liverpool, where they used to go down and meet it and have a good time? These were the people who had originally opposed the making of the canal, and who now fell back on passive resistance.

To meet this state of things the Manchester Cotton Association was formed in November 1894, with Charles Macara as President. It was joined by 265 spinners, with fourteen million spindles, and its main object was to promote the importation of cotton into Manchester by canal. Its success was immense, for within six years the imports of cotton by the ship canal had increased from 64,000 to 550,000 bales. A bale of cotton weighs four hundred pounds.

But Manchester, and, indeed, all the Lancashire cotton industry, was handicapped in another way. In 1902 American cotton-cloth began to invade our Eastern markets in such quantities that Lancashire cotton-makers got badly scared. Mr Macara made inquiries and made the surprising discovery that, although New York was three thousand miles farther from the Far East than Liverpool, the American rate of carriage was about half the English rate.

When Lancashire heard this it was not only the cotton people who kicked, but all the manufacturers who traded with China. Exactly a fortnight after Mr Macara had spoken out a powerful deputation of masters and men called on the shipping companies in Liverpool, and before a month was out the cargo rates from Liverpool to China were made equal with those from New York to China.

More trouble was coming. In 1903 an unprincipled American named Sully started to 'corner' cotton, that is, to buy up all the visible supplies. He did not quite do that, but he came so near it that raw cotton rose to an unheard-of price, and Lancashire manufacturers talked despairingly of closing their mills altogether.

Once more Mr Macara came to the rescue with a plan for shortening the hours of work at all mills instead of closing any of them. Hours were cut from fifty-five to forty per week, the call on the raw cotton was eased, prices dropped, and the unpleasant Sully was smashed and ruined as he well deserved.

"But this may happen again," said Mr Macara. "And we must not let it happen again." So he formed the bold plan of uniting all the cotton-spinners of the world in one great federation, and in the end he and his friends brought into being "The International Federation of Master Cotton-spinners' and Manufacturers' Associations," with a committee that met twice a year in some European city.

This Federation has done wonderful work, work of which very few, except cotton-spinners themselves, know anything. For instance, it took in hand the Indian Cotton-growing Industry. Long ago India produced the finest long staple cotton in the world. It was from this that the priceless Indian muslins were made, and it was estimated that a single pound weight of this wonderful cotton would make no less than 240 *miles of yarn*! Neglect, poor cultivation, bad seed, destroyed the quality of Indian cotton and brought it down to short-stapled, coarse stuff of which the output was only about three million bales. The Federation has not only improved the quality of Indian cotton, but lifted the output from three to six million bales a year.

At the same time it turned its attention to American cotton, which was also suffering from neglect. The yield was falling off, the bales were badly put up. It was, as Mr Macara says, "a most ungroomed and down-at-heel object of commerce." A commission organized by

Mr Macara made a 4600-mile tour of the Southern States, and gave the growers many useful tips as to fertilizing their land, improving the quality of the seed, and storing the bales out of the rain.

This was not the end of the good work done by the Federation. Wheat, like cotton, is an annual crop, and like cotton is grown in many different countries. The wheat-crop may be good in Canada, but bad in the Argentine ; it may be splendid in Australia, but a failure in India. The result was that, since no one even knew how the world's crops would average out, wheat, like cotton, was very much at the mercy of the speculator. About the year 1900 David Lubin, a brainy American, devised a scheme to set up a sort of observation-post, from which all the wheat harvests of the world could be watched, bad results in one continent set off against good in another, and all the wheatfields of the earth kept, as it were, under a single eye. Lubin toured the world with this scheme, but although every one thought it was a very good scheme it did not seem anyone's business to get it into working-order.

At last David Lupin met Mr Macara, and the latter at once turned all his immense energies into making the idea a success. He visited Paris as well as Whitehall, and stirred up the governments of many countries so thoroughly that an International Institute of Agriculture was set up in Rome. A pretty good testimonial to its usefulness is that it was one of the few appliances of peace which survived the Great War.

The International Cotton Federation brought Charles Macara and its Committee into touch with every Government in Europe, with most of the reigning monarchs, with Presidents of Republics, the Khedive of Egypt, the

Governors of the cotton states, and with important people all the world over. King Edward, who was always greatly interested in the cotton industry, invited the Committee to Windsor, where he gave them luncheon. What struck Mr Macara more than anything else was the fact that, although the members of the Committee were of half a dozen different nationalities, yet the King spoke to each in his own language.

For his work on the International Federation Charles Macara was given decorations by Belgium, Spain, Germany, and Italy, and France presented him with the Legion of Honour. England is always a little slow in recognizing good work, but in 1911 Mr Macara became Sir Charles Macara, Bart. What pleased him immensely was that he received congratulations on his baronetcy from working-men all over the north, as well as from his friends among the masters. The secretaries of the two great cotton trade unions—the cardroom-workers and the operative spinners—both wrote personal letters of congratulations in forwarding the good wishes of their members.

In one of his books Sir Charles has written :

> It is a responsibility resting upon those who conduct large industrial or commercial concerns that they should consider it part of their duty to take an interest in all public movements that have for their aim the national welfare.

When the Great War broke out Sir Charles found his hands full indeed, but although no longer a young man—for he was already nearly seventy—he did not shrink from responsibility and very hard work. The Liverpool cotton market is always a sensitive centre, and in August 1914 there were all the makings of a tremendous financia crash. The biggest cotton-crop on record was ready to be marketed, but Germany and Austria, who usually buy in August, were for the moment out of the market. Sir Charles saw that the result must be a glut of cotton and a terrible tumble in its price, ruining growers and distributors alike. He realized that there was only one thing to be done, namely, to close the Exchange. And for a time it was closed, and panic averted.

Cotton keeps. Sir Charles suggested that the best thing this country could do was to buy all the cotton available and store it for the lean years to come. The neutral countries could have been supplied from this stock, and of course we should have had plenty of raw material for making our explosives. The Master Cotton-spinners' Association flatly refused to support Sir Charles's plan. Their only idea was to get their cotton as cheaply as they could. They did get it cheaply, for from seven-pence-halfpenny it slumped to fourpence a pound. But, oh, how dearly they paid later for their short-sighted foolishness, for that same cotton rose later to no less than forty-five pence a pound! When we say that a halfpenny a pound on the world's average cotton-crop means no less a sum than twenty millions you will be able to get some idea of what the nation paid for neglecting Sir Charles's good advice.

Quite apart from the question of price, we could have stopped the flow of cotton into enemy countries, shortened the War by probably two years, and saved the world at large millions of lives and thousands of millions of pounds. This is just one example—but a very good one—of the importance of looking a bit beyond the end of your nose. It also shows how necessary it is to get expert opinion, and how terribly the man or country that will not do so may come to grief. In the long run we had to stop cotton going into enemy countries, but this was not done until nearly the end of 1915.

Another job that Sir Charles tackled was the making of cloth for covering the wings of aeroplanes. He very soon had an ample supply of the finest cloth of the kind ever made. His sensible plan was that the Army and Navy and all the Allies should get their cloth through a single agency, but here again his suggestion was turned down, and a terrible deal of time and money wasted.

Sir Charles has made many friends in his long life, one of whom was the late Andrew Carnegie, a Scot like himself. Starting with nothing, Carnegie became the greatest iron-master in America, and was at one time the richest man in the British Empire. He is well remembered by his libraries, his hero fund, and other charities which still carry on. The two men had this in common. Neither found any fun in piling up money just for its own sake. Andrew Carnegie had an old friend, a blacksmith, who wrote some verses on the subject which will make a good ending for this chapter:

> We're puir bit craiturs, Andra, you an' me,
> Ye hae a bath in a marble tub; I dook in the sea;
> *Café au lait* in a silver joog for breakfast gangs to you;
> I sup my brose wi' a horn spuin, an' eat till I'm fu'.
>
> An' there's nae great differ, Andra, hardly ony;
> My sky is as clear as yours, an' the cl'uds are as bonnie;
> I whussle a tune through my teeth to mysel' that costs
> nae money.

CHAPTER XVI

"HARD WORK THE SECRET OF SUCCESS"

The Story of W. R. Morris

ONE boast which Mr W. R. Morris can truthfully make belongs to no other king of commerce whose story is related in this book, namely, that he is the son of an Indian chief. We do not mean to say that Mr Morris has Red Indian blood in his veins, for he is entirely English. The explanation is this. Many years ago, while still quite a lad, Mr Morris's father emigrated to Canada and went West, where he became driver of a stage-coach. Wild work in those days, when the only white men in the West were miners and ranchers and Indians still took the warpath. The route of his coach ran through Indian territory, and the young driver became so popular with the Red Men that at last they induced him to be recognized as their chief.

But even being chief of an Indian tribe gets tiresome after a while, and in the end Mr Morris, Senior, returned to England, and made his home in Worcester. In Worcester W. R. Morris was born, but he did not live there long, for presently his father moved to Oxford, where his son got his schooling. From his earliest years young Morris had a turn for mechanics, so it is not surprising that when he left school at the age of sixteen he entered the service of a bicycle-maker. The motor-car craze had hardly yet begun, but every one rode bicycles, and the high roads were full of them at week-ends. Little shops were cropping up all along the roadsides, where punctured tyres could be mended and where lamps and oil and various odds and ends were kept in stock.

But a boy of the type of young Morris seldom works long for anyone but himself, and after only nine months in the shop our hero decided to start on his own account. The fact that he was only seventeen, and that his entire capital was five pounds, daunted him not at all. "Hard work is the secret of success," has always been the motto of Mr Morris. "Given the will," he said, in one of his speeches, "one can do almost anything." And by dint of working double tides he soon built up a prosperous little business. Presently he began to make a bicycle bearing his own name, which was so cheap and good that it sold well in the neighbourhood. Not content with push-bicycles, the young designer produced a motor-cycle which was years in advance of anything yet produced, for among other refinements it had a vertical engine and counter-shaft drive.

The motor-bicycle is actually older than the motor-car driven by petrol, for Gottlieb Daimler fitted his first petrol-engine to a bicycle so long ago as 1886. There were motor-bicycles on British and French roads in the very early days of the present century, but they were such crude arrangements that their owners spent more than half their running-time in roadside repairs.

This was the period when motor-cars, having got over their early troubles, were becoming really popular. In 1911 there were 47,000 private cars in use in Great Britain, and the number was rising by ten to twelve thousand yearly. But British manufacturers were still concentrating their energies on what may be called the luxury car. There were practically no cars made of less than fifteen horse-power, and the average nominal power of English-made cars was twenty to twenty-five. Naturally these cars were costly both to buy and to run, and the consequence was an enormous import of cheap American cars, especially of the Ford. At that date there was no car introduced by British makers which gave anything like the value for money offered by the Ford. In power, in hill-climbing, and in cheapness of running there was nothing like it at the price.

Mr Morris, with that far-sightedness which seems the peculiar property of men of his type, realized that there was an immense future for a light car that would be cheap to buy and run, yet powerful enough to carry four people on their business or holidays. He set to work to design such a car, and in 1912, taking his courage in both hands, bought a small factory at Cowley and started manufacturing. There were, it must be remembered, others who were experimenting at the same date with light cars, but these were for the most part ramshackle and quite untrustworthy freaks.

No one but himself knows quite how much work young Morris put into his car. He has admitted that he sometimes worked thirty-six hours at a stretch. Remember, he was then little over twenty years old and—what is the most wonderful part of it all—had little theoretical training in engineering. All he had learned was self-taught, and therefore practical. In 1913 he produced and put on the road the first Morris-Oxford car, a vehicle of the exact size and performance for which the great middle classes were looking—the people, we mean, who could not afford the luxury cars which were being built by all the well-known firms of the time. The quality of these early Morris cars may be judged by the fact that many of those built in 1913–14 are still running at the time of the writing of this chapter, the middle of the year 1928, and that of a consignment of six Morris cars sent to India early in 1914 five were still in active service fourteen years later.

In 1914 came the Great War, and the bottom was knocked out of private motoring. The number of private cars in use in Great Britain dropped from 92,000 to 50,000. During those years the Morris factory was engaged in War-work, and in 1919 when peace had come Mr Morris had to start all over afresh. His thoroughness in the service of his country had nearly ruined him, and when the time came for the instalment of new plant and machinery for the manufacture of his cars he hardly knew which way to turn for the necessary cash. Again it was a case of working night as well as day, and no one with less than Mr Morris's tremendous will-power and dynamic energy could have succeeded in the terrific task before him.

The worst of a man like Mr Morris, from the point of view of his historian, is his incurable modesty. He simply will not describe his struggles. He only smiles and says, " Well, I got through."

He did get through, for at a time when many manufacturers had become slack and casual and were turning out miserably poor cars his were so good that he found an eager public clamouring to buy them. Sales increased, output rose, and even when the great slump of 1920 brought many concerns crashing to the ground the sale of Morris cars was very little affected. Half the industry was bankrupt, and there was a gathering of the survivors to discuss to what point prices of cars could be increased.

W. R. MORRIS 192

Then Mr Morris dropped a bomb by reducing the price of all Morris models. This made him highly unpopular with the other manufacturers, but at the same time brought them into line, forcing them to set their houses in order so as to compete, and the next twelve months showed that Mr Morris alone had the true foresight. For with the reduction in price the demand rose, and whereas in 1920 the output of British cars was only 122,000, in 1921 it jumped with a huge leap to a quarter of a million.

Now the Morris concern forged ahead with a vengeance. The hours of careful thought and the unstinted energy put into the design of the Morris began to tell. Here was the range of cars for which every one had been waiting. Output increased, but the demand ran constantly ahead of the supply. New factories had to be built, and the original tiny building was lost in a huge hive of industry, spreading over more than eighty acres of ground. With the advantage of buying materials in huge quantities a further cut in price became possible without any sacrifice in quality, and for the first time in the history of motoring a soundly constructed, reliable, and economical British-made car was offered to the public at a price which put the American competitors out of the running. By the year 1926 the output had increased to over a thousand cars a week, figures hitherto unknown in the history of British motor-car manufacture, and the number of men employed in the factories rose from 3500 to 4000.

Success never means slackness to a man of Mr Morris's type. Finding that the famous old Wolseley Motor Company was in danger of passing into foreign hands, he bought the whole concern outright for the huge sum of £730,000. Most men would have shied at such a risk, but Mr Morris was confident that his powers of organization could pilot the company safely through its bad time.

Mr Morris also owns Morris Commercial Cars, Ltd., and Morris-Leon-Bollee, one of the oldest firms in the French motor industry, which, like the Wolseley, had fallen on evil days, but has been revived by its new owner's efforts. One more of his many enterprises is the Morris Garages, Ltd., of Oxford, makers of the famous M. G. sports car. The four-cylinder M. G. is probably the fastest standard car of its comparatively small horse-power in existence. A few days before penning this chapter the writer had the offer of a lift in one of these cars from a place in Gloucestershire back to Oxford. The distance was twenty-five miles, the time evening, the road fairly good, but by no means straight. One can only hope that none of the 'speed cops'—as they call them in America—will notice this statement, but if the truth is to be told the little M. G. covered the twenty-five miles in thirty-two minutes, and that without taking any undue risks, for we 'slowed' at every corner, every cross-road, and every village.

No employer realizes more clearly than Mr Morris the need for making his men happy and comfortable. His opinion is that if you pay men well and give them sufficient hours of leisure they can amuse themselves. With money in his pocket and daylight hours at his disposal any man knows where to find health and amusement after his own fashion. This opinion does not, however, prevent the organization of a Welfare Committee, which is certainly second to none.

Although he is now one of the richest men in England Mr Morris works as hard as ever. He takes the keenest interest in the smallest details of his enormous business,

PAINTING A MORRIS CAR

The operators are spraying rapidly as the chassis is rotated.

he lives and breathes motor-cars. Although he has on his pay-roll many highly paid experts in designing and the like he himself remains in absolute control of the design of his own cars, and in spite of the fact that he had no technical training has an uncanny way of putting his finger instantly on the right spot.

Money, as money, means nothing to him, and he and Mrs Morris live in the very simplest style up on the breezy heights of Huntercombe above Henley. Mr Morris is still a young man, one of the youngest whose stories are told in this volume, and there is no doubt but that he will go much farther. He believes that the time has come to develop British trade with the Dominions, and at the time of writing is busily engaged in formulating plans for the extension of his business overseas, having just carried out a personal survey of world markets in a whirlwind tour round the world, covering 37,000 miles in three months.

The accounts of Morris Motors show that for the year 1927 the Company earned more than a million and a quarter on a capital of five millions. Out of this capital Mr Morris himself owns the whole of the two million ordinary shares, yet although there was a balance of nearly a million after paying the preference shareholders Mr Morris refused to take a penny. He put the whole of the balance into the reserve fund. Is there another man in the whole business world who would have exercised such self-denial ?

CHAPTER XVII

THE MAN WHO "STRUCK OIL"

John D. Rockefeller, the Second Richest Man on Earth

THERE is only one man in the whole history of the world who has ever given away £150,000,000 in his own lifetime. And the man who has broken every record for giving away millions, in pounds and dollars, to charities, hospitals, colleges, and scholarships in a dozen different countries began life as a farm-labourer, working fifteen hours a day for 25 cents.

That wage works out in English money at three-farthings an hour. Thirty years later that same man was earning just 64 cents a second and could not stop his wealth growing, until, for the last twenty years or more, he has been easily the richest man in the world, except Henry Ford.

To-day, at the age of eighty-nine, John D. Rockefeller, the greatest philanthropist on record, is known to be worth at least £80,000,000, counting £60,000,000 which he had given in his lifetime to his son, John D. Rockefeller, Junior. One hundred and fifty millions given away, and eighty millions still left! A total amount earned by one man of £230,000,000, or more than the sum produced by the total taxation of Great Britain in one year before the War. How has it been made? The answer, in one word, is "Oil."

It was the discovery of the American oilfields which

turned the farm-labourer into the multi-millionaire, and caused the name Rockefeller to be used as a word meaning immense wealth all over the world. But to realize the real romance of 'John D's' life it is necessary to go back to the beginning.

When John D. Rockefeller was born, in 1839, on a small farm near Richford, in New York State, the family was one of the poorest in the neighbourhood. The farmhouse was one of the most dilapidated imaginable—its roof full of holes, so that the Rockefellers could lie in their beds and gaze up at the stars. Grinding poverty, a constant struggle to make ends meet and to get enough food for the family, was the natural order of things in the home where the future Oil King grew to manhood.

The neighbours, mostly poor farmers, but better off than this poverty-stricken family, were sorry for the family living in the dilapidated farmhouse, and gave them what help they could. But when they found that "little Johnny" was not a bright child—was in fact decidedly dull—they shook their heads and wondered what would become of him.

Having grown old enough to learn the rudiments of farm-work, Johnny Rockefeller followed the usual practice in poor families in America in those days—going to school in the winter and working on a near-by farm during the summer months. Work began at 4.30 in the morning, and continued until darkness came, and the wage paid to him was usually 25 cents a day.

He was grumbled at by the farmers because he worked so slowly. It was an early habit of his to spend some time in laying out a piece of work before he began it. "In this way," says John D. Rockefeller, "I was able to study the best way of doing it." The farmers, however, did not appreciate the forethought and they accused him of laziness. They did not realize that while other boys worked faster they did not perform their tasks so efficiently.

It ought to be possible, when telling the story of the world's second richest man, to say that he loved all work from childhood. But truth must be told, and during those early years, when more fortunate boys would have been at school, Johnny Rockefeller did not like farm-work at all. To-day, looking back on those early summers spent in the fields, he realizes the value of the experience. "It taught me patience," he says.

When still quite a young man, his parents moved to Cleveland, where John D. Rockefeller's first job was to hunt for a post which would enable him to contribute something to the family funds. He secured a post as office-boy with a firm named Hewitt and Tuttle, at a starting salary of between 2 dollars and 3 dollars a week.

It was better paid than farm-work, and more congenial. He was gaining experience of business, meeting people, watching the life of a big city, and gradually discovering his great ambition to make a place for himself in the world. It was during the days as an office boy that Rockefeller made his resolution to succeed, and began to keep eyes open for some idea which would put his feet on the ladder to fame.

During the time of waiting he was training himself for the great career that was ahead for him. And the first lesson which he taught himself was to know how to save—and spend—money. It is John D. Rockefeller's belief that very few people ever learn the art.

" Every young man should take care of his money," he once said. " It is a religious duty, I think, for one to get all the money he can, to keep all he can, and to give away all he can."

Right to this day the Oil King has in his possession a soiled account-book, in which he entered every cent received and spent during those early years. Even then he had embarked on his career as the world's record 'giver.' Between September 1855 and January 1856 he earned just 50 dollars. Out of this sum he paid for his board and washing, and managed to save a little money. Out of his savings he gave a cent to his Sunday-school funds every week, and small sums to other religious causes. Odd coppers, that was all. But they were all he could afford then, and they helped him to form the habit of setting aside part of all he earned for charity, which has since made his name famous.

A year later, as the same record shows, his salary had grown to 25 dollars a month, and he was giving 10 cents to a foreign missionary society and 12 cents to a mission in New York within one month. One of the lessons John D. Rockefeller has tried to teach to others is that you do not have to be rich in order to help a deserving cause, and these entries in a soiled little pocket-book, still treasured, show that he practised as a young man what he preaches as a multi-millionaire.

The next step in 'John D's' career came when he secured a position as bookkeeper in a sewer-pipe business carried on by a Mr Williams at a salary of 1000 dollars a year, equal to about £4 a week in English money. This was real promotion for the man who had started as a farm-labourer, and he was described by his employer as a " quiet, studious, industrious young man, of great energy and keen perception." In fact, altogether a model employee.

The keen perception was there all right, and also the energy, for it was at this point in his story that John D. Rockefeller got the ' big idea ' which made possible his dazzling success.

While working on Mr Williams' books by day he was watching the oilfield pioneers and all their doings in his leisure moments. Oil had then only just been discovered in America, and the quick mind of Rockefeller realized the enormous changes that oil was destined to make in the daily lives of millions, and the wealth that there was waiting for the man who could organize that great new industry.

He studied everything about oil that he could find—how it was located, tapped, shipped, marketed. What it would do, and what the machinery cost. Then, with all the facts at his finger-tips, he went to his employer and proposed to form a partnership to enter the oil-business—Williams putting up the money, and Rockefeller the brains.

Impressed by Rockefeller's insistence that there was a fortune waiting for some one in the ' oil game,' Williams agreed. And so John D. Rockefeller launched out on the career which was to make him the Oil King.

During those first days of the petroleum industry competition was keen, and much of the surveying-work had to be done in secret if oil-bearing lands were to be bought before the news of their value caused a rush of oil-prospectors to the spot. Rockefeller's first task, therefore, was to conduct secret borings in the neighbourhood to discover which districts would yield oil and which wouldn't.

Among the places selected for borings was the cellar of the house occupied by Norman Williams, his partner and late employer. Rockefeller thought that Williams might have been living over a lake of petroleum without knowing it. Oil had been found in various places around, so why not in his partner's cellar? Into the bed-rock of the floor the oil-drill was driven. Rockefeller struck oil all right that day—so violent was the outrush of the thick, oily liquid that the basement was flooded and the house ruined.

Rockefeller was naturally delighted at this rich 'strike,' but Williams and his family were not so enthusiastic. This energetic partner of his had completely ruined his old home, and as Williams was not a poor man the fact that the new oil-well in his cellar meant wealth did not altogether dispel the feeling of disappointment. It was, in fact, largely owing to this adventure with an oil 'gusher' in his own cellar that Williams decided to leave the young Napoleon of the oil-industry to 'go it alone.' The partnership was dissolved, and Williams—the man who gave Rockefeller his first real chance—moved to Chicago, where he continued his original business as a manufacturer of sewer-pipes, eventually becoming a millionaire.

Rockefeller meanwhile continued to 'strike oil' in Ohio and other states until the formation of the Standard Oil Trust, which made him the unchallenged king of the industry and also the second wealthiest man in the world.

It was not easy to become an oil king, not by a long way. Rockefeller worked ten hours a day six days a week for thirty years on end. Once he went ten years without even three days' holiday. Up to the time he retired this amazing man, whose life-story is a series of milestones, each denoting another million dollars given away, had only been across his own country three times, and to Europe twice, and all these trips had been necessitated by business.

The tasks of getting rich and giving money away occupied every minute of a busy life, and Rockefeller gave just as much attention to his charitable activities as he did to making money. He is almost the only man on record who set out to make money—not in order to retire, or to have an easy time, or to travel, but solely because he considers one of the most important duties of wealth is to give as much as possible away. There are so many good causes which Governments cannot assist out of public funds, and which must be helped by wise—and wealthy—private individuals.

Rockefeller's first real holiday was a five weeks' trip across the United States and up to Alaska, undertaken thirty years after that 'gusher' had been discovered in his one-time partner's cellar. During this holiday the then richest man in the world (Henry Ford had not then beaten him in the race for that title) amused himself by talking with the poorest people he could find, by doing all the things which ordinary travellers do, and by climbing a glacier. In all he covered more than 10,000 miles by boat, by railway, and by stage-coach. And five weeks later he was back in his offices and working harder than anyone else in the mighty Standard Oil organization.

To-day, at eighty-nine, his income and that of his family is still about 5*s*. a second. All made out of one fact—that a young bookkeeper did not fritter away his time in the evenings, but studied the oil-industry because there seemed to be a 'chance' in it for a pushing young man. No other idea that ever fertilized the brain of a

JOHN D. ROCKEFELLER, AT THE AGE OF EIGHTY-SEVEN

Photo P. & A.

202

human being made as much money as Rockefeller's dream of a world run on oil, except the dream, told in another part of this volume, of the young man—also a farmer's son—who invented a motor-car which enabled millions to be carried along the roadway by the oil which Rockefeller produces.

Rockefeller and Ford. The two richest men in the world. And each has helped to put the other where he is. There are the two most romantic life-stories of our generation.

John D., as all the world calls the Oil King, has spent the closing years of a great life living in retirement at his country house outside New York, or visiting his family. In his ninetieth year he is a gentle philosopher who loves the woods and the fields, and who has written on nature with a charm that few men could equal.

Apart from the countryside and his family his greatest interest in life is to help the young man who is to-day starting out on a career. Other men have warned the young against borrowing. John D. Rockefeller's favourite text is that a man's sole chance of success in life depends on having money to operate with. "Therefore," says the Oil King, "get the confidence and trust of those people who have money, and borrow." Once he has the capital, according to Rockefeller, it rests entirely with the man whether he becomes a billionaire or a pauper.

John D. Rockefeller has always been an individualist, thinking on lines of his own. Many other successful men do not agree with this advice. "Neither a borrower nor a lender be" is said by many to be the best guide to follow in life. And certainly the reader of this volume will realize, if he perseveres to the end, that whatever may have been true seventy years ago, when John D.

Rockefeller was a boy, it is no longer true to say to-day that success cannot come without money—that is, big capital. It is still possible to found a great business on brains and £100. And it is possible for anyone with brains to save the hundred pounds first. Then, when success comes, it will be all the sweeter because it has been gained without risking anyone else's money.

Whether any idea that could be developed to-day would bring profits totalling £230,000,000—the total wealth that John D. Rockefeller, America's most wonderful old man, has owned in his lifetime—is doubtful. Back in the middle years of the last century a greater chance came to this man than may ever occur again. And although a poor bookkeeper he took it. That is the real lesson to be learned from the life-story of the man who 'struck oil.'

CHAPTER XVIII

THE MILLER'S SON WHO BUILT A WONDER CAR

F. Henry Royce, a Great Engineer

FEW men, even among the really great, have achieved the distinction of seeing a statue erected in their honour before their death. There is one Englishman of our time who can claim to have done so. The Englishman is F. Henry Royce, famous as the engineer who designed the Rolls-Royce motor-car, and the statue, unveiled five years ago, is to be seen at Derby.

A little place called Altwalton, near Peterborough, was his birthplace. Here he was born in 1863 into a humble home, where the wolf was never very far from the door. His father was a miller, who in grinding the corn to provide other people with their daily bread often found difficulty in getting his own.

Those early days were days of poverty, and when his father died the humble home was close to despair. All pretence at education had to go by the board, and young Royce had to put his shoulder to the wheel to help to keep the home going. If you could turn back the hands of time to the year 1873 you might see a little paper-boy darting about the streets shouting the news. That child, ten years old, was F. Henry Royce in his first job. He was selling papers for Messrs W. H. Smith and Son, and the papers he carried gave him a smattering of education, for he read them when trade was slack and picked up a new word here and there.

It must have been a glad day when at the age of thirteen, after a year's schooling, the boy got another job and entered the service of her Majesty's Post Office. He was willing, quick, and alert, and as he took the telegrams to the doors of various houses he strove to do his job better than any other messenger-boy in the service of the Post Office.

A year was spent in delivering telegrams, with spells of dreaming about the future and all he wanted to do in between rush periods. Then he got his first slice of luck. He managed to get into the shops of the Great Northern Railway as an apprentice.

One morning he was delivering telegrams. The next he had handed in his uniform, said good-bye to his fellow-workers, and found himself in a wonderful new world filled with mighty machines.

This was the work he had always longed to do, and Royce decided to be a success if using every ounce of energy and enthusiasm could make him one. So he made himself useful about the engineering works, saying little, but learning all he could. He carried tools, helped to unscrew and screw up nuts, crawled about under and over engines, plunged inside them and helped to disconnect rods, and generally hammered and filed and oiled to his heart's content.

As the reader has seen in an earlier chapter, Henry Ford gained his knowledge of machinery by studying the smallest motors in the world, in the shape of watches and clocks. Royce gained his knowledge by going to the other extreme and studying railway locomotives.

Royce, like many another boy after him, loved engines,

F. HENRY ROYCE

From a drawing by J. Pisani

and with every passing week his knowledge of them grew. Four years at the workshops of the Great Northern at Doncaster provided him with that experience which was the foundation of all his after-achievements.

While he was there he was learning, but he was not earning much. Money was still necessary, so in the end Royce had to leave the works before he had completed his apprenticeship and once more seek fame and fortune in the big world. His chief at the railway gave him a glowing testimonial, shook his hand, and wished him luck. Another chapter in the amazing rise of Royce had closed behind him.

The railway took him to Leeds, where—now eighteen years of age—he set out full of hope to get a job. He went to the nearest works to inquire if they would take him on.

" Sorry, no," they said.

He turned away and made for the next engineering shop, still sure that the excellent references from Doncaster would get him a situation. But again no hands were wanted.

At works after works it was the same story. There seemed to be no room in all Leeds for the boy-engineer who had arrived there with such high hopes that morning.

The end of the day found him tired and still without a job. He bought himself a frugal meal, sought a humble bed, which further diminished his small stock of money, and went to sleep.

The next day he had no better luck. Nor the next. And as day followed day without any sign of work he became more and more footsore and sick at heart.

For a fortnight he trudged round and round the city, while every door seemed shut on him. He would have gone home but for the fact that his reason for coming to Leeds was to earn some money to keep the home together. And all he had done up to date was to spend some of the money—a lot it seemed to the lad—from the tiny store he had brought with him.

Hope was at a low ebb when, at the end of the fourteenth day of searching, he came to the Italian arsenal and applied for a job. The foreman looked at his testimonial.

"All right. You can start at once on machine-tool work," he said.

The young man thanked him and got busy. That was in 1881. He joined the stream pouring into the arsenal and was at his machine when the clock struck six, and throughout the livelong day he toiled, while the hands of the clock crawled round to six again and round to ten. For months he slaved in this manner for sixteen hours a day, and on Fridays he worked all night.

In those days Edison and Swan were still experimenting with the first electric lights that were to flood the homes of the people with light at the touch of a little button on the wall, and when Royce was offered the post of tester with the company that had been formed to introduce electricity to the public he thought his fortune was made. So he came to London, and in addition to working as hard as two men he studied in the evenings under a famous professor who had become interested in him.

He was anxious to learn and to make up for the schooling which he had missed as a boy, and his progress was the measure of his amazing brain. For a whole year he made rapid strides, and at the end of that time his merits were recognized by his appointment as chief electrician to the Liverpool branch of the Electric Light and Power Company.

Having known what poverty was, he had always been thrifty, and when the Liverpool company failed he decided to make a start for himself. For a while he looked around, and then, choosing Manchester as his headquarters, he launched out on his great adventure under the name of Royce, Ltd.

This remarkable young man had already proved himself a splendid electrician, with a knowledge of general engineering and machinery that was so wide as to be very rare, even among older men. The business world realized that fact, and consequently work began to come to him. He did it so well that more followed. Nothing was rushed or badly done—he handled every job to the very best of his great ability.

Wanting to specialize in something, he turned his attention to electric cranes of giant dimensions. He nade improvements not found on any existing type at hat time, and the improvements filled his works with rders. The romance of F. Henry Royce lies in the fact hat his firm are still turning out the cranes that he lesigned to this day, and if you ask those who use them ou will be told that they are as good as the Rolls-Royce ars.

It was the sight of early motor-cars broken down by he roadside which first caused this remarkable British ngineer to take an interest in motor-cars. Having ecided to study them, he was not content with any half leasures. His aim was nothing less than to invent and nake a motor-car which would be the finest ever turned ut in any country. It was a bold dream, even for a rilliant engineer, but he made it come true. While his men were busy building giant cranes Royce settled down to the job of building the first two-cylinder Royce car.

Another young man, the Hon. C. S. Rolls, coming across one of those pioneer Royce motors at a show, was so enthusiastic about this superb production of engineering art that, himself a famous motorist, he there and then undertook to sell all the cars that Royce could build. And so, in 1904, began the partnership between two men, one a brilliant designer and engineer, and the other a famous figure in the motor world, which gave us the Rolls-Royce car, for twenty-five years the king of the road.

F. Henry Royce owes his success to doing his job a little better than anybody else. Nothing but the best would content him. The result was seen during the War, when five out of every eight British aeroplanes were equipped with Royce engines, designed by the boy who had sold papers in the streets of his home village.

It was a Royce engine that drove the first aeroplane across the Atlantic in sixteen hours; another Royce engine that took the first aeroplane to fly from England to Australia.

The famous six-cylinder car which he designed in 1907 made a record that still stands by running 15,000 miles continuously. And all these feats have been made possible by the boy who once trudged the streets of Leeds, hoping against hope that he would get a job of some sort before his money gave out.

Six thousand workers are employed at Derby, where the Rolls-Royce cars are made, and because Derby knows a little better than the rest of the world the true romance of his career, the town set up a statue to F. Henry Royce five years ago.

The story of Royce, king of motor-designers, is a story which bears out the moral that 'a thing that's worth doing is worth doing well.' Whatever Royce undertook, in that work he wanted to be supreme, and he was not content until he had achieved perfection.

His story should give hope to every British boy who wants to handle and make machinery, for there are few poorer than he was in his youth, few who work harder than he worked in the arsenal at Leeds, few who have to study harder than F. Henry Royce studied during his early days in London. And yet the boy Royce lived to become the famous engineer whose designs have beaten every competitor, and whose work has become a hall-mark of excellence in the world of motoring and aviation.

One wonders whether the little paper-boy ever dared guess at such a success as this when he dreamed his dreams waiting for customers in the long ago?

CHAPTER XIX

THE LABOURER WHO EARNED A MILLION DOLLARS A YEAR

The Romance of Charles M. Schwab

ONE afternoon in May 1928 the greatest employers in the British iron and steel industries gathered together at their Institute in London. It was a great occasion. They were there to present the highest honour in their industry—the Bessemer Gold Medal—to an ex-labourer named Charles Schwab, who had started at 4*s*. a day and who had risen to be one of America's greatest financiers and captains of industry.

The story of that career which turned the labourer aged seventeen into the 'Steel King' at thirty-five, and then one of the greatest figures in the United States at sixty-six years of age, reads like a fairy-tale.

It begins in the village of Loretto, in Pennsylvania, where the boy Schwab grew up with a passion for mathematics, chemistry, and engineering. At sixteen the needs of his family necessitated his leaving school, and his first job was to act as relief driver of the coach which his father ran between the village and the nearest railway station.

Next came a job behind the counter of the grocery store at Braddock. Not a very promising beginning for a lad who wanted to be an engineer; but it was a beginning, for at Braddock were the Edgar Thomson Steel Works, owned by Andrew Carnegie, and young Schwab kept his eye open for a chance to doff his grocer's apron

CHARLES M. SCHWAB WITH BESSEMER MEDAL 212

Photo Topical

and get a job in the works. Meanwhile his wage of 30*s.* a week was something like affluence.

For some months he worked hard in an effort to become the best grocer's assistant for miles around. But all the time he had a feeling that one day he would cease to be interested in tins of soup and packets of tea—that he would be handling steel girders and iron rails, building bridges, cranes, and giant buildings.

At last his patience was rewarded. One day the manager of the local steel works came into the grocery store to make a purchase, and Charles Schwab, taking his courage in both hands, asked him for a job.

"Can you drive stakes?" asked the manager.

"You bet," answered the lad. He would have driven bucking bronchos for the chance of getting into those works.

He was taken on to drive stakes at a wage of 4*s.* a day. He worked hard enough to earn twice that sum driving stakes, and at the same time kept his eyes open and learned all he could about the work that others performed.

He showed a natural aptitude for the tasks of organizing and handling men. Six years later the labourer had become the superintendent of the works, then one of the largest in America.

A year later he got another step up in the world. He became chief engineer of the whole Carnegie company at twenty-four, with seven thousand men under him. To realize the romance of this it must be remembered that Schwab had received no technical education whatever. He had never had the money to spend upon taking degrees or attending colleges. All that he knew he taught himself by the method that is open to the poorest boy in the world—by keeping his eyes open.

Not content with a rate of progress which would have dazzled most young men, his next step was to build and equip a new works, the Homestead Steel Works, which he managed himself. At that time the Homestead works was the largest steel-plant in the world, and it was here that Charles M. Schwab instituted for the first time the method of feeding the raw material into the works at one end and keeping it continuously on the move until it came out at the other as the finished product. That time-saving method has since been adopted in more than half the factories in the world, and has doubled the production of steel and many other things as well. But it was new then—and it helped to make America realize that in Charles Schwab the country had found a man who was going to do bigger things than most men.

By 1892 he had become the manager of the whole of the great Carnegie organization. There had been a great strike, and to Schwab fell the task of smoothing over the rankling sense of grievance which it had left behind. He did it, and his reward was the presidency of the Carnegie Company.

In fifteen years the boy who had entered the works as a labourer had got to the very top of the ladder. Even the annals of big business in America contains no more romantic story than this swift rise to fame and fortune.

The British steel-manufacturers had watched his success and decided that Schwab was a man worth 'buying up' to help the British steel industry. One of them offered him an enormous figure to leave the Carnegie company and migrate to Birmingham. Charles Schwab turned it down. Later Andrew Carnegie learned of the incident, and, taking no second chances, he insisted on

Schwab's accepting a long-term contract worth one million dollars a year—the greatest salary ever paid to one man in the history of industry.

That contract figured in an incident which shows how big a man the American Steel King is. In 1900 he set about the task of amalgamating all the principal steel works in the United States in one vast trust, which would have branches all over the world, and be able to execute any order, from a packet of pins to a Dreadnought.

He outlined his scheme to the greatest financiers in the United States, and he won them over. In 1901 the United States Steel Corporation was formed, with Charles Schwab as president, holding nearly £6,000,000 worth of its stock. He was then thirty-nine years of age.

But one thing troubled Mr Pierpont Morgan and the other financiers who carried the scheme through. This was Schwab's contract for one million dollars salary a year. They had never heard of anything like it—the highest salary known was not more than a tenth of that sum.

When Schwab heard of their fears that he might not be worth such a salary he went to Morgan with the precious contract in his pocket and tore it up. He would take, he said, whatever they thought he was worth.

Think of that scene. The ex-labourer, now a millionaire six times over and still young, deliberately tearing up a document which had been worth over a million dollars to him the previous year, and which would have brought him in that sum every year for years ahead. Charles Schwab is the only man who has ever thrown away such a fortune.

Pierpont Morgan realized the size of the man. He actually paid him every cent of what would have been due to him if the contract had not been destroyed.

Schwab lost nothing. But how many men would have done it ?

For four years he remained in office as president of the greatest steel corporation in the world. Then a spell of bad health caused him to resign. At forty-two it looked as though one of America's business geniuses was finished.

Those who thought so did not know Schwab. As soon as he was fit again he forgot all about retiring, and looked round for a task to occupy his time. He found it in a small steel works at Bethlehem, Pennsylvania.

The works were bankrupt when he took them over. It meant competing with the great trust he had created himself. Schwab did not worry about that. Nor did he entice any of the experts who had worked with him in building up the Steel Corporation to join him. He took instead fifteen keen young men out of the mills and made them partners. In other words he gave those fifteen young men the chance which Carnegie, years before, had given him.

Together the sixteen laboured early and late at the task of turning the Bethlehem Works into a paying proposition. It meant taking off their coats and forgetting the clock for eight long years. It meant weathering financial crises when it seemed doubtful whether the works could carry on. It carried on.

Charles Schwab worked as hard as any of them. He put into the business every farthing that he possessed in the world. Then he borrowed all he could and put that in too. If Bethlehem went broke it meant Charles Schwab's selling up his home and starting all over again. That is the sort of risk which the kings of commerce must always be ready to take.

The Bethlehem Works did not go bankrupt. They gradually turned the corner. By 1914 they had become the second largest steel works in the world—the largest was the trust which this same man had created.

Then came the War, and orders began to pour in for munitions and steel urgently wanted by the Allied forces. Charles Schwab cleared every other order out of the way and settled down to the task of working night and day, turning out munitions for the nations which he considered were fighting for the freedom of the world. The Germans, through their American Embassy, offered him a fortune large enough to make any head reel if only he would keep his works on ordinary American orders and refuse to supply Britain and France.

"I told them," relates Charles Schwab, "that there was not enough money in the whole of Europe to make me break my will. I did millions of pounds' worth of business with Great Britain without any contract in writing, and I never had one word of dispute or difficulty or unpleasantness."

The War orders carried out by the Bethlehem Works totalled £100,000,000. It controls nearly half the shipbuilding work of the United States. It employs 100,000 men, and turns out 8,000,000 tons of steel a year—more than the whole steel production of Great Britain.

To have built up such a business would have been romance enough for any man. But Charles Schwab built it up after he had 'retired' at forty-two—after he had already created in the United States Steel Trust the greatest single steel organization that the world has ever seen. One wonders what the worthy grocer who had employed Schwab at 30*s*. a week, if he is alive, must think about it all?

To-day, at sixty-six years of age, Charles Schwab is still fit and active. On the occasion of his visit to London to receive the Bessemer Gold Medal, the highest award which can be bestowed by the steel industry, he revealed his philosophy of life for the benefit of the boys who are facing life to-day.

"Never get mad—it isn't worth it. Be happy. Go through life laughing. Cultivate a happy disposition, and never take yourself too seriously. I don't believe in the so-called great men. I believe the world to be filled with others just as good, if only they get the opportunity."

And about health:

"I am always in bed by 9.30 and up at half-past six in the morning. I don't smoke, and I don't drink—except occasionally for social reasons. I don't object to tobacco, but I just never learned to smoke."

There is the picture of America's steel-king and his career. It is a story which every boy should study, for he had no advantage which we do not all possess, except one. At the moment when he entered the steel industry it was enjoying a period of great expansion. Schwab saw this, and was not content to remain a labourer. He worked all hours, and made himself too valuable to remain a labourer. And there is the lesson of his career—don't be content to jog along in a rut—make yourself so valuable that promotion must come. And if you can, enter a new and growing industry, which will need more and more experts as it grows.

But don't expect to be given a contract for £200,000 salary per annum. No other man has yet received that figure, and Charles M. Schwab received it only because he was worth it.

CHAPTER XX

"BUSINESS IS FUN"

Gordon Selfridge, the Store King

IN this country any well-educated boy can go up for the entrance examination to Dartmouth which is the gate of the Navy, but in the United States a boy must first obtain a nomination from a Congressman. More than fifty years ago a boy named Harry Selfridge was given one of these coveted nominations, and went up for his examination. He passed, then went before the doctors, who turned him down because he was a quarter of an inch too short.

There was another would-be cadet who, knowing that he was too short for the naval standard, went to one of these athletic specialists who do such strange things with the human body and got himself literally stretched into the Navy. In six weeks he had gained half an inch in height, and so scraped through. But half a century ago such things were not thought of, and in any case young Selfridge's family could not have afforded such an expense, for they were anything but well off. Indeed, his father, who had fought for the North in the Civil War, died when Harry was a baby, and his mother was left in very poor circumstances. But Mrs Selfridge was of Scottish descent, and like most Scottish women well educated. She moved from her old home to a place called Jackson in the State of Michigan, and there got a post as school-teacher. In this way she earned enough to keep herself and her little lad, but it is easy to see that young Harry, like so many other successful men, had very few luxuries in his boyhood.

When old enough he went to the public school in Jackson. The American public school corresponds to the English Board Schools. The teaching is free and usually very good. Since the American summer is much hotter than that in England holidays are arranged differently. Those at Christmas and Easter are very short, but there is a three months' vacation in summer. During this time the children do a good deal of work as well as play. Some help on their parents' farms or gardens, others may take an outside job which gives them pocket-money.

Harry Selfridge began to work early. He was only ten when he got taken on as check-boy in a dry-goods store. An American dry-goods store corresponds to a draper's shop in England. He had to carry the bills to the cashier's desk, bring back the change to the serving-clerk, and generally make himself useful. His wages were a dollar and a half weekly—that is a shilling a day—and he evidently made the most of his time, for before the end of that first vacation he was promoted to bundle-wrapper—that is he was given parcels to tie up.

Most of the people in the store were kind to the small boy who tried so hard and did his best, but one or two were sharp-tempered and spoke harshly, scolding him for faults of which he was not conscious. He has never forgotten that first experience. All through the years he has remembered what a glow of pleasure a kindly word sent through his small body, and how on the other hand abuse chilled and unnerved him. And that memory

H. GORDON SELFRIDGE

has made a big difference to thousands of people who have since worked for Mr Selfridge. He never fails to give praise where praise is due, knowing how a pat on the back increases self-respect and how it helps a man or a woman to develop self-confidence. The memory of a boy is very keen, and Mr Selfridge says that he can still call up to mind the picture of that small store, those who worked in it, and their customers. If he shuts his eyes he can almost hear their voices.

Year by year through his school-life he spent most of his summer vacation at work, and there is plenty of proof that he learned a deal of business. One day a boy friend came to him. This boy, older than himself, was editing a small boy's paper, but could not make it pay, and he explained to Harry that he could not get enough advertisements. "Tell you what," said Harry, "I'll take them over, and you shall pay me ten per cent. commission on all I get."

"Done," said the other, and it was done, for by the end of the year the paper for the first time showed a profit. It was only sixty dollars (£12) but enough to allow the two boys to take their first trip to Niagara Falls.

When Harry Selfridge was fourteen he told his mother that he wished to leave school and go to work. His mother objected strongly, vowing that he had much better get on with his education and later go to college. But Harry stuck to it, and in the end had his own way. He got a post in a bank in the town, and though the salary was small, only 20 dollars (£4) a month, the training was most useful, for there, as he says, "I learned the science of figures." The cashier was a nice, friendly person, and invented a way of rewarding the boy for good work. Harry's great ambition was to post the ledger, and the cashier bargained with him that if he went the whole month without making a blot, at the end of that time he was to be allowed to post the ledger.

Harry Selfridge spent two years in the bank, then found another situation as bookkeeper in a factory. But though the pay was better he soon found that there was little chance of advancement, and realized that it was time to make a real move. It was not salary so much that mattered, but opportunity of working up and rising. A big city seemed indicated, and in 1879, a friend having given him an introduction to Messrs Field, Leiter and Co., he decided to go and ask for a job. Departmental firms, now so common everywhere, had their beginning in America, and Field, Leiter and Co. were one of the first. They did a great mail-order business with all parts of the States.

Harry 'landed' a job, not much of a one it is true, for the pay was only 10 dollars (£2) a week, a small sum for a young man to live on in a great town. The work was looking after stock in the basement and keeping stock-books, but it gave a great opportunity to become familiar with all the details of the business, and you may be sure that young Selfridge took every advantage of it. After a couple of years a new chance came his way—an offer to manage a retail store in a Western town. The pay was good, but before accepting it Selfridge decided to consult Mr Field himself.

"You had better stay here," was the answer. "I believe there is a future for you." Young Selfridge took the bull by the horns. "The deputy manager of my department is leaving, sir," he said. "Can I take his post ?"

Mr Field considered a little, then to Selfridge's intense delight said, " Yes."

That was the turning-point, and afterward there was no question of the young deputy manager's leaving the firm. In a year he had risen to be general salesman. Meantime Field, Leiter and Co. became Marshall Field and Company, and developed into far the largest business of its kind west of New York. It was said to be the best-managed store in the West, and its book of rules was celebrated. It consisted of ninety-nine pages, with nine pages of index, and decrees the conduct of employees in one would fancy every circumstance of their existence. Here is an extract:

> It is recognized in this store that the undue urging of merchandise upon customers is not desired, but this does not in any way mean that indifference in the slightest degree is to be permitted. Indifference on the part of salespeople is a very serious blight in any business, and we wish it to be understood that this house considers anything of the kind a sufficient cause for instant dismissal.

Politeness is the first and supreme virtue of the shop-assistant.

> A suggestion comes to us which hardly seems to apply to our salespeople, and especially to those who have been in the store some time. The suggestion is that ladies, in being waited upon by saleswomen, are often addressed, in other stores, as " My dear," or with similar expressions. Any such expressions to customers will be avoided.

When a lady, who is to be addressed as " Madam," not " Lady," wants to be directed to another part of the store, an employee is forbidden to indicate the location " by a careless inclination of the head or an indefinite motion of the hand." The floorman is to be informed, and he, for his part, is particularly instructed to "avoid pointing," and to accompany the inquiring customer to the section she desires to find.

Young as he still was, Selfridge became a traveller for the firm, moving from place to place and interviewing important customers. One day, when waiting in a hotel, he happened to pick up the illustrated catalogue of one of the great Eastern retail houses. Certain points impressed him so much that he decided to go to New York, and when his next holidays were due he went there *at his own expense*. He came back full of new ideas, put them to Mr Field, and at once got fresh promotion to the retail side of the business. From that time he never looked back, but went on from strength to strength. In a year and a half he was head of that side of the business, and within another eighteen months had been offered and accepted an interest in it—that is to say, he became a partner. During the next twenty years life was full and pleasant. Then in 1903 Mr Selfridge, a rich man, though still in the prime of life, decided to retire. He wanted to read books, to collect interesting things, and to be a man of leisure.

He did that for a year, at the end of which he was bored stiff. Business he found was the biggest and best of games, and he determined to go back to it. So in 1904 he bought out the Chicago firm of Schlesinger and Mayer and changed its name to Gordon Selfridge and Co. Under its new head the big shop began to go ahead so fast that older-fashioned firms got scared and combined to buy Mr Selfridge out. They did so, much to the profit of his bank account.

Mr Selfridge had spent several holidays in England,

he liked London, and it occurred to him that there was a fine chance for a new big shop in England's capital city. In 1906 he came over and began looking about. But when he suggested his new idea most people threw cold water on the idea. There was no room for another big departmental store, they vowed, and no place for it. It was certain to come to smash.

But Mr Selfridge, though he knew that he had much to learn about the way in which things are done in London, stuck to his point, and after more than two years of struggle started his new Oxford Street Company with a capital of a million pounds. He decided to have the finest premises in London, and truly his great building is one of marvels. Its foundations are deeper than that of any other in London, for they go seventy feet down into the clay. The walls are twenty-seven feet thick at the bottom, and the floors of concrete are fireproof. The steel-work of the original building weighs three thousand tons. As for the size, it is calculated that if the floors were cut up in sections they would make an area nearly twice that of Regent Street from Piccadilly to Oxford Circus.

The new shop was opened in March 1909, and had 130 different departments, stocked with £400,000 worth of goods. All these could have been staffed twice over, for Mr Selfridge had no fewer than 10,000 applications for posts. To those selected Mr Selfridge gave the advice that under no circumstances should they let a customer leave the house dissatisfied, and to his chiefs of departments he said, " Do your best for the staff, and they will do the best for us."

Thirty years ago the drapery trade in England and Wales was hated by assistants, because, as a rule, they had to 'live in.' They were obliged to have their meals in staff dining-rooms, and very bad meals they were. They slept in dormitories, a number in one room, and had no privacy at all. The pay was very poor, the work very hard, and there were fines for all sorts of small offences. Often an unfortunate girl was fined as much as half a crown for allowing a customer to leave the shop without buying something.

It is not too much to say that Mr Selfridge did more than anyone else to put a stop to this kind of thing. "The basis of all successful business," he says, "is to treat people who work for you, or rather work with you, as you would like to be treated yourself. When a business declines the fault is usually at the top. If I began to relax my interest in the business probably many others would do the same." Another idea of Mr Selfridge's which makes him popular with his people is that he is always accessible to his staff, always ready to listen to their suggestions, and if these are good to follow them up. He says that what people want most in this world is justice and fairness, so no one of his people is ever condemned unheard. Every one gets a fair show.

In most shops the customer has a sort of worried feeling if he or she comes in late. The assistants make the customer feel that customers have no business to be there at or just before closing-time. Mr Selfridge intensely dislikes that 'watch-the-clock' business, and has tried to do away with it. All his people know that, if they want to get off early on any special night, they have only to state good reason, and they will be allowed to do so.

He wants all his staff to get on and do well. "If," he says, "a young man has not earned promotion within three years of his entering our employment there is something wrong with him or with us."

In 1928 the staff of Selfridge's (excluding all branches) numbers just on 5000. They have playing-fields at Wembley, seventeen acres in extent, where all sorts of outdoor games are played, from cricket, football, and hockey to lawn tennis, bowls, and net-ball. There are also dramatic, musical, and other societies, and a rambler group for those who love tramping. Mr Selfridge has a great belief in travel as a means of educating people and broadening their minds, and every year trips are organized for members of the staff to go to Switzerland for winter sports. Parties are also organized for tours through America and Canada. For these they have the rather nice and appropriate name of the "Merchant Adventurers'" parties.

There is no harder worker than Mr Selfridge, but he has one excellent rule of life. "I refuse," he says, "to think of business after the office doors are closed. I refuse to take my office duties into my home and private life—but then I enjoy every minute of business. Business is a wonderful adventure, the greatest fun on earth."

CHAPTER XXI

FROM CABIN-BOY TO WEALTH

Sir Joynton Smith of Australia

THERE can be few healthy British boys who are not at some period of their lives imbued with the spirit of adventure—who long for the chance to go out into the world beyond our shores and seek their fortune :

When all the world is young, lad,
  And all the trees are green ;
And every goose a swan, lad,
  And every lass a queen ;
Then hey for boot and horse, lad,
  And round the world away ;
Young blood must have its course, lad,
  And every dog his day.

The spirit of those well-known lines written by Kingsley has carried many a poor boy across the world to fame. It carried young Rufus Isaacs to India as a cabin-boy. And it carried him there a second time, when he had become Lord Reading, as the Viceroy of our Indian Dominion. It took a young University student to the East, where he became famous as Lawrence of Arabia. And it took another amazing adventurer, General Frank Sutton, out to the civil war in China, where he became Munitions Minister to the Peking Government, the only Englishman to hold such a post.

Fifty-five years ago a British boy, poor in pocket but filled with the desire for adventure, was informed by his father, an ironmonger in the Hackney Road, that he was to "learn the business" ready for the day when he should take it over.

Many boys would have considered the chance to become the owner of a prosperous business a wonderful stroke of luck. But this boy had been dreaming dreams of seeing something of the world, and winning success at something more romantic than ironmongering in London. He considered the position very carefully, and finally decided that, even at the risk of starving in some far-off country, he must escape the fate of being an ironmonger.

There was only one way to do that open to a penniless boy. That was the way Lord Reading first went to India—to sign on to some ship as a cabin-boy.

The ironmonger's son was lucky. He found an Italian fruit ship that wanted a cabin-boy, did two trips to the Mediterranean, returned home to the Hackney Road a hero—and finally sailed a third time as a steward in a P. and O. liner for Australia.

Fifty years later, in 1921, that same boy returned to the Hackney Road for the first time since signing on as a steward of the *Old Pekin*. And he came back as Sir Joynton Smith. In those fifty years he had been President of a trade union and of an employers' federation, built up businesses employing two thousand people, been Lord Mayor of Sydney, the largest city in Australia, and a member of the New South Wales Legislative Council. Like many others he had proved that it is not always true to say that "a rolling stone gathers no moss."

That penniless boy's love of adventure had done more than make him famous. It had kept him young. When young Smith signed on as a steward fifty-five years ago he was said by his school friends to " be handy with his fists." When he returned to the Hackney Road at the age of sixty-five he was still an enthusiastic boxer who claimed to be the champion boxer of his age in Australia. Every day he still spends an hour in his gymnasium. But we must get back to the beginning of his adventures, because it was the qualities of courage, enterprise, and resource which young Smith showed in his early struggling days that made his success possible.

Before Smith found his first job he spent several fruitless weeks hanging round shipping offices in search of it. He did not get one in that quarter, but he learnt one valuable piece of knowledge, which was that before you can go to sea you must produce a discharge paper.

Here was the first 'snag,' but his Cockney resource saved him. Two days later he was the triumphant possessor of a discharge paper for a voyage from Bombay, which he had bought from a deck-hand for 1*s*.

Armed with this, he secured a position as engineers' servant on a Mediterranean fruit boat of 300 tons named the *Burlington*. She was what was termed a " weekly ship "—that is, the crew were paid weekly.

Conditions in those days were vastly different from those of to-day. The first wages which young Smith earned on the road to fortune were 8*s*. a week, out of which he had to provide his own food, while a full-blown sailor was paid only £4 a month, out of which he had to keep a wife and children ashore and contrive to feed himself whilst at sea. How they managed to live at all upon this wage was one of the mysteries which Smith had to solve while he was an engineers' servant on the *Burlington*.

His duties on the first trip consisted of scrubbing out the engineers' quarters, keeping them tidy, and cooking their food.

He had never cooked a meal in his life, so the first thing he did was to inspect the store cupboard, which contained the victuals for the voyage. The store cupboard did not look promising. It only measured three feet by two feet, and into this was crammed the food which the engineers apparently considered sufficient for a voyage to Naples, but which would have been considered scanty for a day's cruise to any cook on shore.

The stock consisted of bags of rice, sago, tea, sugar, and a few other common household commodities, all lumped together, and in the case of the sugar and tea already mixed up in one heap.

Smith had, of course, stated that he was experienced as a sea-cook in order to get the job, but the captain's cook, who as the senior was entitled to use the galley first, soon discovered that he wasn't.

"How he discovered that much was amusing," Sir Joynton Smith told the writers. "I had been washing over the floor of the engineers' cabin when the cook came in and pointed out that I was wringing the water out of the floor-cloth shore-fashion instead of sea-fashion. I never learnt what the difference was, but as that cook was a sport and kept the information to himself it did not matter."

He speedily discovered that his 'speciality' in cooking was pancakes. It was not the usual menu on board that ship, but Smith served them up three times a day, until there was nearly a mutiny on board.

Then it was that he sought the advice of the captain's servant, who showed him how to make 'dry hash,' a dish consisting of sea-biscuits softened in water and fried in fat. The result at first was terrible to look upon. It was more like 'try hash' than 'dry hash,' but after much practice he eventually concocted a dish which could be taken to the table.

The *Burlington* ran down the Channel to Swansea, where they loaded patent fuel for Naples, the outward-bound port of destination.

Smith made two trips to Italy on the boat, and then returned home to the Hackney Road. There all his small acquaintances turned out to greet him, and for the first time he knew the satisfaction of having done something. He regaled them with stories of sea-serpents and orange-groves, taking care not to mention the cockroaches which formed by far the largest part of the ship's population, and which, it had often seemed to him, cultivated a particular fondness for the engineers' quarters immediately he went on board.

After a few weeks at home the wanderlust gripped him more strongly than ever, and he signed on as a steward in the P. and O. liner *Old Pekin*, bound for Australia and New Zealand.

The first glimpse of the latter country so thrilled him that he decided to stay there until he had either found success or grown tired of travelling. So he left the *Old Pekin* and secured a position as bedroom steward on board a small coastal boat, the *Tampo*.

In the days that followed he sailed in ships with millions of rats on board. At least Sir Joynton Smith declares to-day that there must have been millions of them. On these Australian coastal boats it was a common thing for the crew to sleep on the decks, with no bed and no pillow except those which they made out of ' shore rugs ' and pieces of tarpaulin.

Occasionally the stewards, as a special favour, were allowed to sleep on the settees in the passengers' dining-room. It was to this favour that Smith owed the loss of some of his hair.

Hair-oil being unknown on board, the stewards used salad-oil as a pomade. One night, when curled up on a narrow settee, Smith awoke out of a deep sleep to find a number of rats eating the salad-oil off his hair, and managing to eat a fair quantity of his locks as well in the process. After that salad-oil was no longer used as hair-cream on that boat!

Five years of that life, cruising up and down the shores of New Zealand and Australia, in a climate which was often perfect and occasionally stormy, and Smith had become chief steward and also President of the Seamen's and Firemen's Union at Wellington, New Zealand, a body which had been formed to get some of their grievances redressed.

During these years at sea Smith was saving money, spending his leisure hours watching the water slipping past—and thinking out the next move on the road to fortune.

His chance came about ten years after he had left London, when, with three hundred pounds capital—his entire savings—he took an hotel in Wellington as his first business venture.

That decision was the turning-point in his life, for it saw the day dawn when he stopped working for a wage and started working for himself. Nothing that has happened since in the life of Sir Joynton Smith would have been possible if he had not possessed the courage to become his own master.

Fortunately the hotel proved successful, and after some years he sold out at a profit and went to Sydney, where he took another hotel which was reported to be doing badly, and therefore going cheap.

He ran this long enough to discover that there was no valid reason why it should not do well, and then bought it. Success was steadily coming nearer. In a year or two he had bought a second hotel with the profits made in the first. A few years later he was definitely established as the proprietor of a string of hotels in New South Wales.

In those early days as a hotel proprietor the experience which he gained at sea stood him in good stead. It was his boast that there was no job in all his hotels which he could not do himself if occasion demanded it. Indeed, upon one occasion he spent a day in his kitchen in order to renew his acquaintance with making puddings, and no one who ate the dinner that night in the dining-room above knew that the 'pudding cook' had been given the night off!

His next adventure was to buy a racecourse. At least it was not a racecourse when he bought it, but a large tract of land situated within twenty-five minutes of the Central Post Office in Sydney, which had been used as an old reservoir since the days of Botany Bay.

Having bought it, the next task was to drain it. Several engineers were consulted and declared the feat to be impossible, but at last an expert was found who could do it, and the Victoria Park Racecourse rose out of what had been a swamp.

The work took eighteen months to complete, and the

weekly wage-bill during that time was £800—paid by the man who had arrived in Australia as a cabin-boy. To-day the racecourse is one of the finest in Australia.

When it was finished he became interested in the Blue Mountains, the great tourist-resort in the hills about sixty miles from Sydney, and which is as popular among holiday-makers from that city as Brighton is with Londoners or Blackpool in the Lancashire district.

There he built yet another hotel and lit it with electric light made on the premises. Soon after it had opened the town asked Mr Smith whether he could supply electric light to the public, so he enlarged his works, and electric light came to Blue Mountains.

Then a second town asked if he would supply them with electric light. And another. The end of it was that he was supplying electric current to a string of towns stretching for forty miles, and his little electrical plant, built to supply one hotel, had grown into the largest private lighting-plant in Australia.

There followed two steps further on the road to fame, which had not been on his original programme, thought out during nights at sea under the Southern Cross. He started a weekly newspaper, and entered politics.

The paper, which was appropriately christened *Smith's Weekly*, to-day has a large circulation in New South Wales, while shortly after his entry into municipal politics Mr Smith was appointed Lord Mayor of Sydney, the town for which he has done so much. It was for his work in that office during the War that the former cabin-boy from the Hackney Road was knighted.

Three years after the War Sir Joynton Smith came back to England for the first time since signing on as a cabin-boy. And he came back as an example of what enterprise and endurance can accomplish.

While in London he visited the Hackney Road and saw the ironmonger's shop which was owned by his father and which his family had hoped he would carry on.

It was from the Hackney Road that he used as a boy to walk to his work at Waterlow's, the printers, before he went to sea. Work in those days was from 8 A.M. until 8 P.M., and his wages 2*s*. 6*d*. per week. If you were a minute late in the morning you were locked out for a time, and a proportionate amount of money 'docked' from your 'salary.' His father, when young, worked even harder. He had been a brass-founder, and his hours were from 6 A.M. until 8 P.M., and he had to walk about five miles to his work.

Yet it was this early Spartan training that laid the foundations to the success which Sir Joynton Smith has since achieved. Those early experiences taught him the value of money, and proved very helpful when it came to handling men in after years. It helped him to avoid many of the mistakes which so often cause friction, where only a hearty co-operation between master and workman should be found.

But the greatest lesson of all his adventures, in Sir Joynton Smith's own words, is just this:

"My advice to youths who are perhaps becoming restless, and who yearn for 'other fields to conquer,' just as I did fifty-five years ago, is to remember that, while England is the place for dreams, it is in Australia where dreams come true. And never forget that the goal of ambition should be the day when you stop working for a wage and start working for yourself."

CHAPTER XXII

FIRST WITH THE NEWS

The Story of W. H. Smith—and Son

RATHER more than a hundred years ago two brothers ran a small stationer's shop in Duke Street, Grosvenor Square. They were Henry Edward Smith and William Henry Smith, sons of Henry Walton Smith, who had come from South Devon to London some thirty years earlier. The sign over the door was " H. and W. Smith, Newspaper Agents, Booksellers, and Binders."

Henry Edward was an indolent, easy-going man, a complete contrast to his younger brother, who was at work in the shop early and late.

In those days newspapers were desperately expensive. There was a tax of fourpence on each copy, so that most papers cost the buyer sixpence, and of course very few were sold. Two or three people would unite to buy one copy, and it would pass from hand to hand for several days. The great cost of newspapers gave William Henry Smith the idea of starting a reading-room, where subscribers might see a number of papers, so premises were rented at 192 in the Strand, where, for a guinea and a half yearly, patrons could see no fewer than one hundred and fifty newspapers besides magazines.

The venture paid well, and the profits enabled the brothers to launch out as stationers, travelling-case and pocket-book makers. But the elder brother did not like all these novelties, so in 1828 W. H. bought him out and ran the business by himself.

In those days the Post Office did not send out its country mails till the evening, so London papers were already twelve hours old before starting on their long journey by mail-coach to the Provinces, and if a customer lived more than a hundred miles from London his paper was at least forty-eight hours old before he got it. W. H. thought he could do better than this, so he started a service of horsed carts to collect the papers from the printing offices, and sent them off by the early day coaches. Sometimes a coach started before the papers arrived, in which case Smith's well-horsed cart galloped after it, and the papers were flung aboard. When the news was very urgent the drivers were instructed to get relays of horses and deliver the papers themselves. On one occasion—when George IV died—Smith's actually chartered a special boat and delivered the news in Dublin twenty-four hours ahead of the sleepy Post Office.

As soon as trains came into use W. H. took every advantage of the quicker service, and as early as 1847 employed no fewer than nine special engines to carry papers to the North. In 1848 he was delivering newspapers in Glasgow at a speed of fifty miles an hour for the whole journey. They got there two hours before the Post Office mails had even started from London.

W. H. had married in 1817, and at first he and his wife lived over the shop in Duke Street. When he took the new premises in the Strand he moved to rooms in the upper part of the building, and there in the year 1825 W. H. Smith the second was born. His father had never forgotten the old home in Devonshire and sent his son to

THE FOUNDER OF W. H. SMITH AND SON

238

be educated at Tavistock Grammar School. Tavistock lies just on the south edge of Dartmoor, and young Smith and his friend William Lethbridge fished in the Tavy and wandered over the heathery moor. His headmaster was his uncle, the Rev. William Beal, his mother's brother. W. H. Smith, Junior, was a quiet, hard-working sort of boy, and it was his ambition to become a clergyman like his uncle.

But the work in London was growing too much for his father, so the boy gave up the idea of the church and went straight into the business. He began at the bottom, but did so well that in 1847, when he was twenty-one, his father made him a partner. That is how the great firm of W. H. Smith and Son came into being.

Father and son worked tremendously hard. They had moved their home from the Strand to Kilburn, and every weekday, summer and winter, they drove down at four o'clock in the morning, took their coats off, and worked with their men packing and dispatching papers. "First with the News" was their motto, and they certainly acted up to it. *The Times* was so pleased with their work that its proprietors gave out that up till 6.45 in the morning they would supply W. H. Smith and Son only, so that every one who wanted *The Times* early in the morning had to go to them for copies.

Their old premises proved too small for the ever-extending business, so in 1849 the firm moved from 192 Strand to 136 in the same street, and three years later to 186. Later these buildings at 186 were enlarged, and more recently the great new Strand House in Portugal Street was built on the site of the old King's College Hospital, which was moved to Denmark Hill.

1846, the year in which young W. H. became a partner,

was long known as the year of the railway mania, for the country went mad on building railways. Hundreds of small railway companies came into being, all of which were gradually bought up by the present large concerns. The early railway carriages were little better than horse-boxes—not so good as some modern horse-boxes. No cushions, no light, no heat, bad springs ; and the stations were no better. The companies made no attempt to provide food either for body or mind. When there was a bookstall it was usually kept by some disabled porter who sold cheap sweets and penny bloods.

In 1848 the younger Smith happened to hear that the bookstall at Euston Station was vacant, and it suddenly struck him that here was a new opening altogether. Why not take it and stock it with up-to-date newspapers and good reading matter ? Worth trying anyhow, he thought, so he rented the stall for something under one hundred pounds a year. The stall was opened on November 1, 1848, and passengers quickly showed how much they appreciated the change. So did the railway companies, with the result that during the next fourteen years W. H. Smith and Son started bookstalls at every important station in England, Wales, and Ireland.

In those days there were very few novels, and what there were used generally to be published in three volumes at half a guinea a volume. Realizing that precious few railway passengers were going to pay a guinea and a half for a work of fiction, Smith's decided to publish something cheaper, and that is how the famous half-crown 'yellow-backs' came into being. Mrs Gaskell's *Cranford* was the first, then the firm bought the copyright of Charles Lever's novels, *Charles O'Malley*, *Harry Lorrequer* and others. These went like wildfire, and the demand very soon drove other publishers to produce equally cheap books. Having proved that there was a market for cheap fiction, Smith's did not trouble to publish any more.

Indeed the firm had their hands full with other matters, for in 1851 the first great London Exhibition was opened, and with it came the beginning of modern advertising. Thousands of people arrived from the colonies and abroad, manufacturers and tradesmen wanted to advertise to travellers the goods they had for sale, and it was suggested to the railway companies that the walls of their stations were the best for the display of advertisements. You can hardly imagine a railway station without advertisements, yet up to 1851 the walls of all stations were bare, except for a few time-tables. The companies agreed that it was a good idea, but they could not be bothered to paste up posters, so announced that they would let the sole right of using their walls to anyone who would make arrangements with the individual advertisers.

Once more W. H. saw a chance and took it, and so was born the Railway Advertising Department. The first contract was with the London and North Western, but success was not so sudden as in the case of the bookstalls. In 1854 there was a profit of only £130 on an expenditure of £9800. But after that the new venture began to bring in big sums every year.

W. H. Junior was by this time one of the busiest men in England. In 1854 his father became ill, and though he still drove daily to the office could not do much in the way of business. In 1858 he decided to retire and leave his son in sole charge. He went to Bournemouth, where he lived the last seven years of his life.

In that same year, 1858, W. H. Junior married Mrs

Leach, a widow, daughter of Mr Danvers, who was clerk to the Council of the Duchy of Lancaster. Now that his father had retired and he himself had a wife, he decided that his work was too much for any one man, and began to look about for a partner.

He chose that same William Lethbridge who had been a school-fellow of his at Tavistock and was at this time a master at St Paul's School in London. With Mr Lethbridge's help he was ready to start a new business—that of supplying books on loan to people in country districts. It is said that he was not keen about this new departure. Certainly he did not foresee that it was going to grow into the biggest thing that his firm had ever done. The station bookstalls were the distributing centres for the lending libraries, and continued to be so for nearly half a century.

What caused the change to the present shops was the steady increase of rental demanded by the railway companies, so that in 1905 it was decided that the contracts with the Great Western and London and North Western must be ended. The question was what could be done. It was out of the question to allow more than two hundred bookstall managers and their staffs to be thrown out of employment, and to abandon all the business so carefully built up. "Perish the thought!" said the partners. "We will start a shop in every town where formerly we had a bookstall."

So the bookstall managers set out to find shops, and as soon as a suitable one was found and leased the shop-fitting department came in and worked at top speed to fit it up. The whole change-over was made in the astonishingly short time of ten weeks. Ninety per cent. of the old customers came to the shops, and in many

THE FIRST SMITH BOOKSHOP 242

cases found the shop more convenient than the bookstall. Then, too, there was so much more room in the shops that the firm were able to offer many things, such as stationery, which could not have been sold from the stalls.

But we are jumping ahead too fast, and must go back half a century or so. W. H. the elder had long wished that his son should stand for Parliament, and Mr Lawson, afterward Lord Burnham, of *The Daily Telegraph*, told Lord Palmerston that there was a young man in the Strand who would one day be heard of. In 1865 the younger W. H. stood for Westminster, but was defeated. Three years later he tried again, and this time got in with a good majority. His fellow M.P.s laughingly called him "Old Morality," but he became very popular, and though no great orator always spoke straight to the point, and showed so much sound common sense that the leaders of his party soon had their eyes on him.

He first made his mark in the House by a Bill for securing the Embankment Gardens, which at that time were about to be covered with public buildings. Every Londoner must be grateful to him for saving this beautiful open space. In 1874 Mr Disraeli, who was then Prime Minister, made Mr Smith Financial Secretary to the Treasury, and in 1877 he became First Lord of the Admiralty. It is this appointment to which Mr W. S. Gilbert refers in the famous song, *The Ruler of the King's Navee*, in the comic opera *H.M.S. Pinafore*. In 1885 Mr Smith became Secretary of State for War under Lord Salisbury, and at the end of that year accepted the terribly difficult post of Irish Secretary. On the 23rd January 1886 he went to Dublin to be sworn in, and only two days later the Government was defeated and resigned. A very few months later Lord Salisbury came back to power, and W. H. Smith became First Lord of the Treasury and Leader of the House of Commons. A big jump indeed for the Tavistock Grammar School boy, yet it is safe to say that no promotion was ever better earned.

There is a limit to the work any man can do, and in 1891 W. H. was taken ill and obliged to retire from public life. He was appointed to the ancient and honourable office of Warden of the Cinque Ports, and spent the last few months of his life at Walmer Castle, the Warden's official residence. This castle has walls no less than sixteen feet thick, and is one of the most wonderful buildings in the South of England. There he died in October 1891, and Queen Victoria created his widow Viscountess Hambleden, the title being taken from the village near Henley where her home, Greenlands, was situated. W. H. had been offered a peerage during his lifetime, but had quietly refused it. He preferred to die as he had lived, simply Mr W. H. Smith.

His successor was his son, the Hon. W. F. D. Smith, the late Lord Hambleden, but by this time the business had grown far beyond the capacity of any one man to manage, and there were several partners at its head. We have mentioned first Mr Lethbridge. He remained a partner until he retired in 1886, but since he never married had no one to succeed him in the business.

The next was Mr Charles Awdry, another West Country man, a native of Wiltshire. He was a Winchester boy who started life as a barrister, but W. H. had his eye on him, and in 1870 took him into the firm. He became a partner in 1876. A fine cricketer and oarsman, it was he who started the W.H.S. Cricket club, and did more than anyone else for the athletic side of the big business.

He was a partner up to 1911, and his eldest son succeeded him.

A great business firm swallows men of all professions. Mr Lethbridge was a schoolmaster, Mr Awdry a barrister, and the next recruit, Mr A. D. Acland, an engineer. He had been trained in the railway works at Swindon, and had actually helped to build London's first Underground railway, the smoky old Inner Circle. He came into the firm in 1885 and married the late Lord Hambleden's sister. His experience as engineer made him very valuable to the firm, and outside the business he was for many years a keen volunteer and Territorial officer.

Smith's is the largest business house in England that remains a private partnership, but there is good reason for this, for if it were converted into a public company there would always be the danger that one of the great publishing houses might get a controlling interest. Once that happened the firm's reputation for fairness and impartiality would be at an end. Smith's have always been proud of this reputation, and in the matter of books and papers it has been their policy to favour no one. In a little book issued in 1855 and called *General Rules to be observed by those engaged at the Railway Bookstalls of W. H. Smith and Son* appears this rule :

> Particular care is to be taken that no daily paper is mentioned by name at the carriages, but the boys are simply to call " London or morning papers." On no account is one paper to have preference over any other.

That tradition has been kept up ever since.

At present the business is so huge that it would take whole chapters to give any real idea of its various branches. With about a thousand shops and stalls all over the kingdom the supply departments have to be on a simply colossal scale. Just to give a few examples, the firm uses six hundred tons of wrapping paper yearly for newspapers and parcels, while an average of three tons of string is consumed every week. Think of the miles of string in a ton ! Yet half a ton is used every working day. The stalls and shops get through a million and a quarter envelopes a year, while the Post Office is paid £2500 a month for the stamping of wrappers used in the newspaper department.

There are all sorts of what may be called side-shows. For instance, books need rebinding, and the firm have their own department where 1200 books a week are rebound. There is also a fountain-pen hospital, where first aid is rendered to 60,000 pens a year.

The main departments are of course all under separate roofs and separate management. The biggest is the library. Of a new novel by a popular author as many as two thousand copies may be ordered, and the total stock amounts at any time to over a million separate volumes. Surplus copies are sold at reduced prices, some being rebound, some merely cleaned, but some that are too far gone are destroyed. In some years as many as sixteen thousand books are sentenced to destruction. The printing works, situated near Waterloo Bridge, are gigantic and issue about fifty weekly or monthly publications. The machinery hall alone has an area of twenty-five thousand square feet. In the works department all the new stalls are built, and fixtures and fittings stored, from stalls complete and ready to be sent out down to the iron hooks on which advertisement boards are suspended from the station walls.

The firm still uses a large number of horses for distributing

THE RIGHT HON. W. H. SMITH
Photo Elliott & Fry, Ltd.

papers in London. At the stables in Kean and Water Streets the bill for oats alone runs to £5000 a year, and the stables have their own smithy. At Kean Street many of the horses live *upstairs*, the stairs being represented by a sloping path covered with thick coconut matting, leading from floor to floor.

The oldest department and still the most important in the business is that of newspaper-dispatching. More than a century ago the first Mr W. H. Smith began the work with only two helpers; to-day five hundred men are employed who work in shifts all the week through from Monday to Saturday, coping with the ceaseless rush of morning and evening newspapers, and periodicals of all sorts.

But although the packing goes on throughout the twenty-four hours the busiest time is still the early morning, when the masses of dailies, *The Times, The Daily Mail, The Daily Express, The Daily News*, and the like, come pouring in. With these the margin of time between the moment they arrive and the moment at which the carts must leave to catch the newspaper trains is always short. It must be calculated in minutes, almost in seconds. The rush begins about half an hour after midnight, and lasts for about five hours.

In the great packing-room at Portugal Street are rows of long tables behind which men stand at regular intervals. As the dailies come in from the printing-office they are distributed in piles, each man being responsible for supplying the correct number of certain papers for each of the thousands of parcels.

The wrappers are ready beforehand, great sheets of brown paper. On the outside of each sheet is pasted the address-label, on the inside a printed list showing exactly how many copies of each newspaper that particular branch requires. So many quires of *The Times*, so many of *The Morning Post*, so many of the *Sketch* and *Mirror*. As each man puts in the proper number of his particular paper he pushes the parcel to the next man, who in his turn slides it to a third. At the far end of each table stands a checker who sees that each bundle is correctly filled. The bundles then go to the tiers-up who secure them with a special 'Smith' knot, and are run out on trolleys to the fleet of waiting cars and vans. The moment a van is filled off it goes, racing through the empty streets for the station.

In another part of the same building the postal section are hard at work wrapping the newspapers which have to be sent by post. The wrappers are ready addressed and ready stamped. A third department is busy with contents bills, making them up into bundles for the newsagents. Contents bills are only next in importance to newspapers in the eyes of the newsagents.

The number of newspapers sent out daily by W. H. Smith and Son exceeds a million, and to this must be added a million periodicals. Twelve million separate papers weekly take some handling, and explain the terrific bill for paper, string, and postage to which reference has already been made.

The first W. H. Smith had very strong ideas about keeping the Sabbath, and for nearly 100 years it remained a definite rule with the firm that no work shall be done on Sunday, so in spite of the tremendous increase in the number of Sunday papers Smith's did not handle them. Years ago the firm received a command to supply a number of the Royal Family with certain newspapers, among which was *The Observer*. Smith's wrote to say that since *The Observer* was a Sunday paper, and since the firm did no Sunday trading, they were unable to supply it. The next thing was a visit from an indignant official who could not understand how the rule of a firm of newsagents could stand in the way of a Royal command. Smith's were polite, but firm, and the Royal personage had to purchase his *Observer* elsewhere.

Even W. H. Smith and Son have, however, been compelled to conform to modern Sunday conditions, as owing to increased Sunday traffic the railways have in some instances insisted on the opening of the bookstalls on that day.

CHAPTER XXIII

THE MAN WHO MADE BUSINESS AN ADVENTURE

When Opportunity Knocked for Angus Watson

IT is commonly suggested that opportunity knocks at least once at the door of most of us. This chapter, however, is concerned with the history of a young man upon whose door opportunity knocked not once but twice. When in the early twenties the chance of making a great position for himself in the United States came his way he refused the offer because "home is best," "burned his boats," and returned to England. As it turned out it was the first step to success—but at the time was looked upon by all his friends as a mistake. However, he was a fortunate young man, which is merely another way of saying that he worked hard and long, and possessed more than the average amount of determination, vision, energy, and enthusiasm.

On his return to Newcastle-upon-Tyne opportunity knocked a second time, and the manner in which he dealt with the occasion is the story that we have to tell. In less than twenty-five years Angus Watson, the young man referred to, built up a great business in this country, and added his name to the long roll of pioneers who risked everything for their dreams, but who finally won through.

Those who, like the writers, have examined the careers of modern business-builders are repeatedly struck by the

ANGUS WATSON

fact that it is the boy who in the early days faced difficulties and adversity who eventually succeeds to the big positions in the service of business, industry, or the State. This is not to say that big organizations have not been founded by men who were wealthy from birth ; more often than not, however, will it be found that the origin of some national, or even world-wide, organization can be traced to one or two individuals, who in their early days had hardly two pennies to rub together, but who possessed something more precious than the proverbial " silver spoon."

The dreamer of dreams, who has the energy, determination, and the pertinacity to carry them out, surmounts all obstacles, and never doubts that the goal will be reached. Countless examples of this principle are all about us—Strathcona, Carnegie, Ludwig Mond, Cadbury, Massam, to mention only a few—and in this case Angus Watson, the founder of a big business.

Angus Watson was born at Ryton-on-Tyne on January 15, 1874. His father and mother, both descendants of Scottish Covenanters from the ancient " Kingdom of Fife," held closely to the Puritan outlook on life, and brought up their family, so far as moral and religious teachings are concerned, very little different from the principles under which a boy three hundred years ago would have obtained his first impressions of life.

He attended his first Sunday School when barely three years old, and like other boys as he developed took his share in, and no doubt enjoyed, the vigorous outdoor pleasures of the modern boy—Rugger, bathing, cycling, and similar outdoor sports.

His father died at an early age, and he was left with the responsibility of immediately turning his hand to business, with a view to adding his quota to the support of his family. On his own initiative he left school before he was fifteen years of age, and made immediate application in his native city for four different positions, which were at that time advertised as available.

The first was in a coal-exporting office, the second in a wholesale grocery business, the third with a firm of drysalters, and the fourth with a corn merchant. He selected the grain business, and commenced there on the frugal salary of 5*s*. a week.

It was hard work, for he began business in the morning at 8.30, and frequently carried on until nine o'clock at night. At the end of twelve months something more remunerative had to be discovered, and he accepted a position as bookkeeper with a commission agent in the canned goods trade at 9*s*. a week. The fact that he had never studied bookkeeping, and knew nothing of the trade that he was taking up, did not deter him, for he argued that bookkeeping could be learned in the evenings, and, further, that if he kept his eyes open he could soon learn the elements of the business that he had chosen. He was destined to remain in this trade for twelve years, and to gain there an experience that was to be of great value to him later on in life.

Progress is apt to be slow and difficult for the boy whose initiative is held in check by his dependency upon the contents of his weekly pay-envelope. Angus Watson would have risked his own comfort, even his future, for his dreams, but he could not risk his mother's welfare—he therefore plodded on, ever on the look-out for the next move onward.

By the time he had reached eighteen years of age he had worked himself up to the position of salesman with a firm dealing in imported canned goods at Newcastle-upon-Tyne. One morning, during the course of an interview with one of his customers, he was shown a tin of Norwegian brisling, a small silvery fish caught in the northern fjords, akin to the sardine family. An old ship's captain from Stavanger had brought over to this country an experimental consignment of Norwegian sardines packed in olive-oil. The occasion and the man had met—that small tin of fish shown by a friendly grocer to our young salesman implanted the seed of a great idea in the mind of a future king of commerce. He succeeded in persuading his firm to allow him to try out the possibilities of the northern 'sardine.'

His first visit to Norway followed, and there he negotiated for a supply of brisling, and arranged a definite contract with one of the Norwegian sardine pioneers (who happily is still alive to-day) for the delivery of one thousand cases in the year. An amusing story is told of his first purchase of a silk hat and frock coat with a view to making up at least in outward appearance for his lack of years and experience. The hat no doubt played its part in impressing the canner, but it was 'matter under the hat' which counted, inasmuch as he was successful in bringing the fishermen and canners to his way of thinking, and, what is more, has enjoyed their confidence and affection from that day to this.

Back in England, a salesman again, he took the high road north and south, visiting every large town through-the country, and at the end of his first series of visits his order-book showed that his idea as to the potentialities of a big market for canned fish in this country was correct.

He has told the story of his first day in London,

arriving late at night, without knowing either the names of the streets or a single customer in that great city—he confesses to having felt lonely, and although buoyed up with faith in his idea almost despaired of making an impression on the ' city of millions.'

His first day's work in London resulted in only four small orders ; what was more important, however, he obtained the head-office addresses of several companies which controlled a large number of branches. Further, he was fortunate in being given the buyers' names, and information as to the days upon which they could best be seen.

Here let us relate a story which reveals the importance of little things in life. His interview with his first big buyer produced little, until when packing up his samples the unusual nature of the buyer's name caused him to remark, " Forgive me for mentioning such a personal matter, but your name reminds me of a well-known cricketer, whose averages I used to study when I was a lad at school."

" Oh, indeed," replied the one and only—Spofforth. " Well, I am the man."

It turned out that the ' demon bowler ' had married the daughter of the founder of the business during one of his visits from Australia, and at that time was the actual proprietor of the company. After an encouraging smile and a chat about cricket the buyer turned to the sample again, and to the delight and surprise of the young salesman placed an order for a case of brisling to be sent to each of 160 branches.

More was to follow—a personal introduction to another important buyer was arranged by the friendly Australian. This prospective buyer controlled an even larger number of shops. As a result, the total of the day's work amounted to nearly 800 cases—one example at least where cricket and good business went hand in hand.

In the few years immediately following a new article of food appeared on the British table. Our young business man, however, soon began to look round for further fields to conquer. Realizing that business practice was changing, he got into touch with one of the most progressive firms in the country at that time—Levers, the soap-manufacturers—and ultimately left Newcastle to join their staff.

Angus Watson is able to look back and to point to a series of milestones in his business career. Soon after joining Lever Brothers he obtained his first important promotion, and reached a definite turning-point in his life. The story of what he did when he got there is worth retelling.

Stamfordham is a little hamlet in south-west Northumberland—a charming spot in the summer, but very much off the beaten track in the winter. The little village was practically snowed up during a certain winter early in the nineties of the last century—even the mail was unable to get through, and practically all traffic on the high country roads was stopped by deep snow-drifts.

Much to the surprise of the local grocer a young salesman called upon him one morning when every one else was either safe indoors or employed in cutting a way through the drifts. On hearing the story of the traveller's successful efforts to reach Stamfordham—the young salesman was from Newcastle—the grocer was so astonished at his pluck and determination that he there and then made out an order for every single line on the salesman's list.

This order was reported in the ordinary way, and happened to catch the eye of the sales manager, who ultimately reproduced it in detail in a circular for the rest of the sales staff. Mr William Lever—as he then was—called for the details of such an exceptional order, and only then were the conditions under which it was entered made known.

In consequence, very shortly afterward the young salesman—still in his early twenties—was promoted to the position of manager of the company's Glasgow office. After further experience in Hull as branch manager he was selected for important work in the opening up of his company's business in the state of New York, U.S.A. One more milestone in his career had been reached—still another loomed further ahead.

The story of his next promotion is very similar to the Stamfordham incident, and resulted in an equally important step forward. In visiting Courtland, New York State, he approached all the important wholesale merchants, with a view to a purchase of his new line of soap, only to find that they were entirely without interest in the British product. Nothing daunted, he proceeded to convince the shopkeeper—the person who comes in actual contact with the public—that he had a product worth their consideration. As a result of his work and the handing over of the orders to the surprised wholesalers he was able to fill his book with bulky orders for the men who had just a little while before refused his original offer.

The Courtland orders again came to the notice of the chairman of the company, and at the unprecedented early age of twenty-eight the boy from Tyneside was offered the presidency of the Lever Company in San

Francisco, at a salary which even to-day would be considered large. The early years of hard work and unflagging zeal brought him the enviable position of being in close association with one of the leaders of British industry. Lord Leverhulme, as he ultimately became, and Angus Watson developed a close friendship, one which it has been a pleasure and inspiration for others to observe—a case almost of 'David and Jonathan' over again.

Opportunity on this occasion was knocking loud at the door—the vista of commercial success on an exceptional scale opened up to the man who a short time before had known real poverty. The majority of us surely would have accepted the position—Angus Watson refused the offer, resigned from his company, and returned to 'canny Tyneside.'

Two reasons prompted his action; he wanted to build up a business of his own in his own country, and although some years had passed he had not forgotten the sample tin of Norwegian sardines which was shown to him by the friendly Newcastle grocer.

Turning his back on a great opportunity, to the surprise of his colleagues, and, if the truth must be told, to the dismay of his old chief, he faced his new future, and realized that the moment for putting his early dreams to the test had actually arrived. Having crossed the Rubicon, he left working for others behind, and decided that he would build up a business for himself, or lose every penny of his savings in the attempt.

About this time he formed a friendship which was destined to become one of the most potent influences in his life. He met Henry B. Saint, who was afterward to become his business partner, and the two together invested a total capital of £2000 in the new enterprise. It is worth noting that since his first situation in a corn-merchant's office he had practised the art of saving—at first only a few coppers a week—later a fair proportion of his total earnings. By this time these had amounted to the round sum of £1000, and this gave him his first opportunity. The friendship thus started with his colleague, Mr Saint, a man some fifteen years older than himself, has continued without interruption for over twenty years, down to the present day.

We of the British race always have a warm corner in our hearts for those who tackle the forlorn hope—the adventurer who invests his last penny in a chance against great odds. The spirit of the Elizabethans, the courage and vision of a Clive, a Livingstone, or a Rhodes, finds its outlet to-day mainly in the world of business, and is none the less real because applied to business-building. The adventure into which Angus Watson plunged on his return to England called for just the same pluck, vision, and endurance as that which has helped to blaze new trails in other spheres of life.

A small warehouse, hardly more than a room, was taken in one of the side-streets of Newcastle, and "one man and a boy" were engaged. In January 1903 the trio, giving themselves the dignity of a firm, commenced the task of creating a new British industry! Whitman's clarion call, "Henceforth I ask not Good Fortune; I am Good Fortune," was chosen by Angus Watson in these early days as his own personal motto. How closely he has lived and worked to this his present position in the industrial life of the country amply typifies.

The importing firm with which he had in previous

years been associated in Newcastle had made little or no progress following his initial venture in the sale of brisling. Certainly the results were not promising enough to indicate to any but the long-visioned that the young man had taken the right step in throwing up the presidency of a great company in the United States for a small warehouse in the cloth-market of Newcastle-upon-Tyne. The little silver fish, however, were his dream, just as wrapped, labelled, and "better soap" had been the vision which prompted William Lever, and motor-cars Henry Ford, to launch their small craft on the turbulent waters of the industrial world.

A second visit was paid to Norway, where arrangements were made, not only for an alteration in the size of the can, making it more suitable for the British market, but also in the quality of the contents. The packers realized that the young firm had at its head some one who possessed considerably more initiative and energy than the average, and in consequence they gave him every help and support in his new work. It is typical of the man that in arranging the new contracts with the canners he insisted upon his old firm in Newcastle enjoying the same favourable terms as himself.

The combination of a first-class article, modern selling methods, and hard, unremitting toil resulted, in the short space of two years, in seeing the small company established on a sufficiently firm basis to enable him to consider in 1905 his first big advertising contract totalling one thousand pounds.

The well-known 'Old Salt' trademark is so closely associated with 'Skippers' that it is probably not generally known that some little time elapsed after the founding of the business before this trademark was used. One day Angus Watson happened to notice in a photographer's shop in Nottingham a wonderful photograph of a picturesque old fisherman. Like a flash came the great inspiration 'Skipper Sardines!' As a result of negotiations the sole copyright of the photograph changed hands for a matter of a few pounds. This trademark to-day is conservatively estimated to be worth a quarter of a million pounds.

Later Angus Watson got into touch with the original, who turned out to be a man of the name Duncan Anderson—a retired Naval seaman. For some years he had been employed as a model for artists and photographers; now his picture as a trademark on a tin of sardines became world-famous, so much so that artists no longer wanted to paint him purely for 'art's sake'! Thus was born one of the most famous trademarks of the world. Anderson remained on the pay-roll of the company as a pensioner until the day of his death, which occurred just after the War—and his grandson was about that time taken on to the Company's staff as salesman.

The next big step in Angus Watson's story was the birth of 'Sailor' salmon slice, the second great venture in 'ready-to-serve' foods. This business, which was first of all developed with British Columbia salmon, has now almost entirely gone into the Far East, where the Company and its associates market the whole output of salmon from those waters.

Gradually other classes of 'ready-to-serve' foods were added, until to-day the house of Angus Watson, founded by a lad who had started with no advantages except energy and honesty, is one of the largest distributors of 'ready-to-serve' foods in the world with a capital of £2,000,000.

In 1921 another dream of Angus Watson's, that of being an actual canner and manufacturer, was realized, a factory being organized in Newcastle for the manufacture of all kinds of delicacies preserved in tin and glass. The new enterprise cost one hundred thousand pounds at the outset—a lordly figure by comparison with the small beginnings of the parent firm some twenty years earlier.

In the enormous growth of the Company the original 'Skippers' were by no means neglected—the 'fish' upon which the business had been founded and built are still sold in thousands of shops all over the world, so much so that to-day the bulk of all the Norwegian brisling packed is each year handled by this English firm. Thirty-eight years ago, when the first contract was placed by the young salesman of eighteen for a thousand cases, the entire production at that time hardly exceeded two thousand cases—to-day the output runs into millions per year. Thus the founding of a new business in Newcastle-upon-Tyne meant prosperity for the Norwegian fishermen, more work for those engaged n the home distributive trade, and at the same time a new delicacy for the British housewife.

Truly a great achievement! Many men have received high honour for doing less—one honour alone has Angus Watson accepted. The late King Oscar of Norway, with the consent of H.M. King George V, conferred upon him the Order of St Olaf for his services in the stablishment of the Norwegian brisling industry. At he same time the accompanying offer of British knighthood was firmly but respectfully declined. Angus Watson has not sought the limelight, and certainly never will. His title to fame is in the organization which he has built—the army of happy and prosperous employees associated with him.

The following interesting figures give some idea as to the results achieved by twenty-five years of business pioneering :

1903.	Capital ..	£2000	Total turnover in packages, approx. ..	25,000
1927.	Authorized capital ..	£2,000,000	Approximate sale in packages	75,000,000
1903.	Number of employees....................			2
1928.	Approximate number of employees, including those engaged in associate companies and canning abroad			10,000
	Profits distributed over the period among employees, including Nominal shares amounting to £50,000, approximate			£80,000

Angus Watson is not a proud man—no one is more unassuming, but this surely is lifework in which any man might take legitimate pride.

What is the greatest lesson that life has taught this business-man ? Here is Angus Watson's reply to that question :

> All that I have learned brings me to one conclusion—that the three qualities requisite to all progress are character, courage, and the ability to work hard. With these three qualities, success—and I use that word in its fullest meaning—is inevitable. The laws of life are not difficult to understand, although obedience to them is by no means easy. They are that a man gets what he gives, and that self-enrichment can only always be the fruit of self-discipline. Success is not accidental—it is the invariable outcome of well-directed effort and a clear vision of the goal to be achieved. The man with a ' silver spoon ' in his mouth is suffering from an added handi-

cap, for Nature never gives with one hand without creating corresponding disabilities with the other. Believe in yourself, have faith in the ultimate decency of life, and have courage to face and to overcome difficulties.

Thus the faith of a business-man, and to it might be added :

Achievement is but another milestone along the highway of progress—the end of the journey lies ever beyond.

CHAPTER XXIV

THE WORLD'S GREATEST STOREKEEPER

Frank W. Woolworth of the U.S.A.

NOTHING over ten cents. There are probably few towns of any size in Great Britain or the United States in which that sign is not known, and hardly a single house which does not contain some article bought at Woolworth's Stores, the amazing multiple-shop business which has a turnover running into tens of millions of pounds annually—all made by selling articles at the price of sixpence or less.

The story of Woolworth's is in many ways the most romantic of all the epics of business success. This great string of shops, numbering over 1650 in America and over 320 in Great Britain, was started and carried to success in the face of enormous difficulties by a farmer's boy — almost penniless, almost friendless, possessing nothing at first but a belief in himself as a salesman, and a dream. That dream was the dream of whole shops devoted to selling many different things cheaply, and before he died the farmer's boy had lived to see it come true, and to build the highest skyscraper in New York—the Woolworth Building—out of the profits from those millions of sixpences which flowed into the cash-registers of the stores he had founded.

The story of Frank Woolworth, and his 'craze' for starting a 'sixpenny store,' is one that should be learned by heart by every boy who stands at the beginning of his career. No finer story of success won from failure against all the odds of poverty and lack of influence has ever been told. When he has read the story we are now going to tell, no boy will be able to say any more that he has no chance of success. For if anyone ever faced real hardship without a chance to get out of the rut it was Woolworth. And he died a millionaire and a world-famous man. All made on sixpences.

He was born on a farm at Rodman, New York State, and his parents moved to Great Bend, another district of the same state, when young Frank Woolworth was seven years old. His early years were a time of hard, grinding poverty of a sort which would have killed all hope in any boy of less courage and less belief in himself.

"We were poor—so poor that I never knew what it was to have an overcoat in that terribly cold climate," Frank Woolworth told Mr B. C. Forbes, who has devoted part of a book to this remarkable life-story.[1] "I never knew how to skate, because I had not the money to buy skates. One pair of cowhide boots lasted a year, or rather six months, for the other six months I went barefooted."

When not at school he worked on the farm, but all the time his thoughts were wrestling with the great problem of how to take the first step upon the career which he dreamt about—getting a job behind a counter.

Schooldays behind him, he took winter courses at a business-training college before actually beginning the search for work.

One would imagine that in a rapidly growing community, such as the United States was at that time, there

[1] *Men Who Are Making America* (B. C. Forbes Publishing Co., $3).

would have been plenty of employers who would have jumped at the chance of engaging a boy as keen as young Woolworth. But it is sometimes difficult to make another man realize how capable you are, and Woolworth did not find the task any easier than do most poor boys anxious to make a start in life.

After days of walking from store to store in the towns within driving-distance of the farm he was still workless. He persevered—the whole story of Frank Woolworth is the story of perseverance—and in the end he got his first chance as assistant station-master, without pay, at the local railway station.

You will ask what such a job had to do with selling anything. In the early days of 'one-horse' townships in the United States the station-masters often carried on 'side-lines' in addition to their railway duties. The station-master at Great Bend was one of these. His 'side-line' was keeping a small grocery store in the freight-shed attached to the station, and Frank Woolworth took the job because it meant the chance of really selling something for the first time.

The 'takings' at this grocery store averaged only a few shillings a day, but it was a beginning, and while there he was getting to know the people who travelled by railway, and looking for something better at the same time.

Eventually he found his first real job as a salesman, at the age of twenty-one. This was in a clothing-store in a near-by town, and to get it Woolworth had to agree to work for three months without salary—a condition which was only possible because he possessed fifty dollars, the laboriously scraped-up capital of ten years' work on the farm and at odd jobs.

F. W. WOOLWORTH

To keep that job meant living on three and a half dollars a week for three months, and then, when his capital had gone, upon the same sum received as wages. It was a fearful risk, for if he were not kept on after his money had run out, he would have to go home penniless.

But Woolworth realized that the boy who means to succeed must take risks, and he took them. On a March day in 1873 the future millionaire drove away from the farm on a sleigh. There was snow on the ground, it was bitterly cold, and he was perched up on a sack of potatoes that his father was taking in to market. Thus he started out on the road to fortune.

At the end of two and a half years he was earning six dollars a week and becoming an experienced salesman. Hearing of a better job going, he applied for it, and was taken on at ten dollars a week.

It was a princely wage, but he had to earn it. His new employer was a tyrant, and at times Woolworth was terribly depressed. After two months the man reduced his wages by two dollars a week. The disappointment, added to the impossibility of pleasing his employer, preyed on Woolworth's mind. It ended in a nervous breakdown and a whole year at home, during which he was unable to do a stroke of work.

On the strength of this last job—and a wage of ten dollars a week—he had married, and after his illness so certain was he that he would only be a failure in business that he bought a small farm and with his wife started raising chickens, vegetables, and anything which seemed likely to enable them to pay their way and provide the balance of the purchase-money, which he had been given time to find.

Four months later the first firm he had worked for

sent for him and offered him ten dollars a week to return to their store. That offer may be said to mark the turning-point in Woolworth's life, not because of the salary offered, but because this recognition that he had been successful as a salesman in their clothing-store gave him back confidence in himself.

Leaving his wife to look after the farm, he went back to the store. Later they let the farm and took a small house close to his work. A year later he had saved fifty dollars and was the father of a bonny child.

Life was still hard work with no pleasures. Woolworth earned his ten dollars a week, for he worked behind the counter from seven in the morning until ten or later at night. But he was gaining experience—the experience which, in 1879, was to enable him to launch out for himself. It was in that year that he first put his dream of a five-cent (or threepenny) store to the test by opening his first shop at Utica, New York State.

The idea had been tried out in a small way in the shop where he was employed. Some trays filled with various articles, labelled 'All at five cents,' had sold like wildfire on market-days, and Mr Moore, Woolworth's employer, advised his assistant to carry out his intention of opening a whole shop devoted to five-cent articles without delay.

The trouble was money. Woolworth had not enough saved to stock a store, and said so. Whereupon Mr Moore offered to let him have credit to the extent of about £70 worth of five-cent goods.

Thus the first Woolworth store came into being—and failed. The craze for 'nothing over threepence,' which had flared up, died out, and Woolworth returned to Mr Moore disappointed and disheartened. Luckily for

Woolworth his former employer still believed in him, or this chapter would never have been written.

He lent Woolworth more stock, and a second store was opened at Lancaster, Pennsylvania. This store was an instant success, and when, after the public interest in 'one-price' stores died out, all his competitors had closed their doors Woolworth's second attempt continued to flourish.

A third store was opened, and his brother installed as manager, but this, like the first, failed and was closed down. What greater romance of business could there be than this simple fact, that of the first three Woolworth's stores—the first of nearly two thousand which exist to-day—two out of the three failed completely. Yet Woolworth remained confident that he would succeed. It was a bad time for store-keeping. A great many shops that had taken up the 'nothing-over-five-cents' idea were closing their doors. But he had faith in himself, and that faith was justified. Soon only Frank Woolworth remained.

By 1880 he felt rich enough to take the first holiday of his life, and he returned to his 'home town' to find himself a hero. From that moment he might have left a large part of his work to others, but Woolworth never slackened off. He knew that if his success was to continue it was safer to continue to work hard himself—and so he worked. There are few instances on record of lazy men getting anywhere, and he knew it.

A fourth store was opened at Scranton, in Pennsylvania, and to this went his brother as manager. The brother is now a millionaire, and the Scranton store is still one of the most prosperous.

This further success emboldened him to open a large

shop in Philadelphia itself, but here he had to admit defeat, and in a few weeks the store was closed down after making a loss of about £100. Three out of the first five Woolworth's stores had proved failures. The average man would have said that the outlook wasn't too hopeful. But the farmer's boy who had worked for the love of selling knew better. He had two prosperous shops—and he meant to have a thousand. So he went straight on, opening store after store, and installing in each a member of his family, or some trusted employee as a partner. In this way he was able to ensure that the stores were well looked after.

It began to look as though the battle were won—as though the days of failure and struggle were over. But then came another check. He opened a store at Newark, another large town, and it failed. So did another attempt. Still believing that success was just round the corner—and determined to persevere until he won it—he tried opening 'shilling stores.' Again he met with failure. But by this time failure meant nothing to him. He remembered that 'the man who never makes a mistake never makes anything else,' and so he went on trying out every idea that sounded possible. Often he lost a lot of money, but always some store or other would 'boom' and restore his depleted capital in time for the next experiment.

Step by step he built up his chain of stores, and at last came the moment when he felt justified in opening a tiny office in New York, from which he could buy stock for all the shops. He did not aim at anything very large—Woolworth never made mistakes like that. Just one room costing a few shillings a week rent. Here he worked fourteen hours a day, doing his own bookkeeping,

THE WOOLWORTH TOWER, NEW YORK 270

thinking out new schemes, buying stock for his shops, planning new stores. No man could work so hard and keep fit, and in the end he broke down and had eight weeks in bed.

From this point he began to see that the time had come to let his staff take over some of the work. He had laid the foundations of a great business, now it must be kept going by others, while Woolworth himself planned ahead. The farmer's boy had reached the day when he could think in terms of head-offices, travellers, managers—and ever more and more stores.

In ten years he had established twelve successful shops, all containing not a single article priced at more than sixpence. He had overcome his early failures, and he had opened and stocked those twelve shops without borrowing a penny apart from the original stock of the first two shops, supplied on loan by his late employer.

The thirteenth store should have been unlucky, according to superstition, but it wasn't. It was the biggest of all up to that date, at Brooklyn, just outside New York, and it showed a profit from the start.

'Nothing succeeds like success.' A branch office was opened at Chicago, and more stores opened their doors in the Middle West of the United States. By 1905 Frank Woolworth was able to register the business as a private company valued at £2,000,000. And this, remember, all built up from one shop stocked with goods worth £70. By 1912 the number of Woolworth stores had grown to 600, and the company was beginning to extend its operations to London and other parts of Great Britain.

By 1916 he had become the largest trader in the world, serving 700,000,000 customers every year, who spent the amazing sum of £20,000,000—all in sixpenny articles. His staff exceeded 50,000, and his stores numbered over a thousand on both sides of the Atlantic.

Nothing like this had ever been known before. And behind the giant business organization loomed the giant Woolworth Building, the highest skyscraper in New York.

The Woolworth Building was built by Frank W. Woolworth to be a world-wide advertisement for his 'nothing over sixpence' stores. Those millions of sixpences which poured over his counters provided the £2,500,000 which it cost to raise the pinnacle of the building 792 feet above the New York streets. And the man who had made it all possible was a farmer's boy who was too poor to have an overcoat in the bitterly cold winter weather. In all the stories of successful men there is none which reveals more clearly the reward of perseverance, of enthusiasm, and of hard work than this.

Since 1916 the Woolworth Stores have gone on growing. There is now an English branch of the company guiding their interests here, and over 87 per cent. of all the goods sold in the 320 British stores are manufactured within our own shores.

There is no need for us to detail any of the articles which you can buy in these shops, they are too well known. In the United States alone Woolworth's stores have sold 50,000,000 pairs of stockings in a year and 90,000,000 pounds of confectionery. In fact, there is one factory in America which works twelve months in the year, with the most modern machinery, making one brand of toffee for the Woolworth shops.

After those figures remember the boy who rode to his first job sitting on a sack of potatoes, and you will see that business can be romantic.

CHAPTER XXV

BUILDING THE FASTEST BOATS ON RECORD

The Romance of Sir Alfred Yarrow

WHEN, on January 13, 1842, Alfred Fernandez Yarrow was born in London, it is very improbable that even his parents—whatever dreams they may have had about their boy—foresaw that one of the greatest pioneers of the nineteenth century had arrived in the world.

They had not, however, long to wait for the first signs of that creative genius which has since turned the London schoolboy into one of the greatest characters in the story of British shipbuilding, for Alfred Yarrow was only eight years old when he perfected his first invention.

An elderly aunt, Miss Lindo, frequently required help in winding her wool, and to Alfred fell the duty of holding the skein on outstretched arms while the old lady wound the wool into a ball. Now this duty prevented Yarrow from getting busy with more interesting pursuits, so he invented an automatic wool-winder for his aunt, which delighted the lady and enabled him to escape a task which did not seem suitable for a growing 'man.'

As he grew up, he showed more and more interest in mechanical things, not always with the happiest results, for when a boy begins to experiment, he does not fully understand that strange happenings are liable to occur. One evening, for instance, he attached a small air-pump to the gas-pipe in the workshop set aside for him in his home and forced air into the gas main. The natural result, which Yarrow did not foresee, was that the gas so treated would not burn, and forty or fifty houses in the neighbourhood were temporarily plunged into darkness. The 'breakdown' was followed by a special investigation by the company, but, perhaps happily for the youthful experimenter, the trick was never discovered.

Equally devastating—and perhaps more comic—was Yarrow's first experiment with electricity, then the new force which had fired the imagination of every boy.

Aided by a school friend, he placed an iron shutter under the mat near the kitchen door. This they connected by a wire with the outside of a Leyden jar, while a further wire connected the handle of the kitchen door to the inside of the Leyden jar. The two 'experimenters,' having fixed their apparatus, waited patiently for something to happen. They did not have to wait long. The cook, on her way to the kitchen with a tray of glass and china, paused on the mat and grasped the handle of the door. At the same moment the conspirators connected the switch so that a complete circuit was made and the current of electricity passed through the cook's body. The experiment was a terrific success in more ways than one, for the startled cook, being thus introduced to electricity for the first time, dropped the trayful of glass and china, and the two boys, realizing that discretion was the better part of valour, fled to the coal cellar and remained there until matters were calmer.

Pranks such as these might annoy his parents, but they also made them realize that Alfred Yarrow had more than ordinary talent. When, therefore, the opportunity occurred to apprentice the boy to Messrs Ravenhill, marine engineers, for five years without premium, the opportunity was seized, and at the age of fifteen and a half Alfred Yarrow left school and was launched upon a career destined to become one of the most dazzling successes of our times.

The work of the firm consisted almost entirely in constructing engines for naval vessels, and during the next five years Alfred Yarrow went through the pattern shop, foundry, turnery, and drawing office.

While learning the mysteries of marine engineering, Alfred Yarrow and his friends continued to carry out experiments on their own account in his private workshop. One of these, a mechanical contrivance made with the assistance of a friend named Hilditch, was an apparatus for cutting up oranges. In those days home-made marmalade was popular, and the news soon spread that Mrs Yarrow's delicious marmalade was made with the aid of a machine invented by her son.

This little contrivance, which, it was rumoured, could cut up in five minutes enough oranges to supply a whole family for a year, brought Yarrow his first taste of fame, for before long trays laden with oranges were being brought to his home with a request in each case that " the young gentleman " would be good enough to cut them up.

The biggest success achieved by these two boys, however, was not the invention of an orange-cutter, but the erection of the first private overhead telegraph in London. The story of this really amazing achievement may best be related in the words used by Lady Yarrow in the interesting book which she has written on her husband's remarkable career,[1] and from which many of the facts contained in this chapter were taken.

[1] *Alfred Yarrow: his Life and Work* (Edward Arnold, 5s.).

At this period very little was known by the public about the science of telegraphy. In attending the Juvenile Lectures at the Royal Institution, Yarrow had the opportunity of seeing some Wheatstone instruments exhibited by Faraday. Taking them as a guide, Yarrow and Hilditch created a complete telegraphic installation between their homes. The little apparatus, which they made without any assistance, cost only 2*s*. 6*d*. (excepting the expenditure on the copper wire which connected the houses).

It is quite certain that the telegraphic connexion between the houses of the young friends was the first private wire used in London. The erection of the overhead wires caused some consternation, and there was a good deal of difficulty in obtaining the necessary permission for passing the wire over the property of various householders. One old lady said she knew all about telegraphs, and was perfectly well aware that the wire would destroy her wall very shortly. Another neighbour called to complain that she could not sleep for thinking of that dreadful wire above her house. Another lady said that the lightning played on the wire all night, and sent a lawyer's letter, which resulted in a different route being taken, although the wire in its original position only passed high up over a corner of her garden.

Again, permission was refused for the wire to be fixed to a chimney-stack until a written statement was sent by the fire insurance authorities to the effect that no danger existed and that it would not invalidate the policy.

At last, however, every one was appeased, and the telegraph completed, after which it was in daily use and a great success. We have not the space in this chapter to include the very interesting details explaining the apparatus used by Yarrow and Hilditch, but these appear in Lady Yarrow's book, and boys (and others) who are interested can by reference to that volume construct for themselves a private telegraph on exactly the same lines as the one with which these two boys made history.

SIR ALFRED YARROW *276*

Photo Lenare

That Yarrow's telegraph was a striking achievement is proved by the following letter, written to a London newspaper by a resident of Holloway at the time:

> In your impression of yesterday you give some particulars of the electric telegraph from the premises of Messrs Waterlow & Sons on London Wall to Birchin Lane, remarking that it is the first instance of the construction of an electric telegraph for private purposes. Allow me to correct this statement, for there has been for three or four months past, in the road in which I reside, an electric telegraph extending about the same distance as the one you mention.
>
> It is entirely the work of two school-boys and communicates between each other's houses, crossing two public roads: but what I wish more particularly to call attention to is the small cost of this telegraph, not amounting to many shillings, which renders it likely that such an apparatus will come into general use.

At the end of his apprenticeship with Ravenhills, Yarrow found that the outlook was not bright. His father had lost his capital in a copper-mine in Cornwall, so there was no possibility of help from his parents. And Ravenhills offered him a seat in their drawing office and £100 a year with a 'take-it-or-leave-it' air which caused Yarrow, full of ideas and energy, to decide to leave it.

He was twenty-one when he turned down that offer from his old firm and set about the task of thinking out the next step.

As we have said, he had plenty of ideas, but before those ideas could be developed, tools were necessary, and one cannot buy tools without capital. His problem was settled by two kind offers of help, one from an aunt and the other from a friend of his father, which put him in possession of a capital of £400. About the same time, a firm of agricultural engineers who were developing a steam plough invented by Yarrow and Hilditch, decided to open a London office to push the plough and offered Yarrow £100 a year to take charge of it. With this salary, £400 in the bank, and a small income from royalties and patents, and occasional payments for drawings and designs, Yarrow began the greatest adventure of his life and launched out on his own.

The first big engineering problem which engaged his attention at this time was the invention of a steam carriage which would travel along the roads with speed and safety. With the help of Hilditch he got to work, and in 1861 the Yarrow-Hilditch steam carriage was invented and taken up by T. W. Cowan of Greenwich.

The first steam carriage was tested between Greenwich and Bromley, a distance of ten miles, once a week, late in the evening. It was completely successful, although the apparition, belching smoke and flames from the funnel of the boiler, frightened sundry old ladies as it passed by their houses.

Unfortunately during one test the steam carriage, when travelling at twenty-five miles an hour, frightened a mounted policeman's horse. The man was thrown, breaking his leg. It was this accident, among other causes, which led to an Act of Parliament being passed forbidding the use of steam upon the road, unless carriages were preceded by a man carrying a red flag, a law which stopped the development of this type of vehicle until, years later, the internal combustion engine arrived and the law was altered.

About this time, Messrs Coleman, the agricultural engineers whose office he looked after in London, and who were selling his steam-plough, made him a preliminary offer of a partnership. The arrangement fell through, much to Yarrow's disappointment, yet but for this piece of bad luck, as he then considered it, Yarrow might have spent the whole of his life as an agricultural engineer, and his later successes might never have happened. Once more we see how little things in life may shape our destinies.

After two years as the London representative of Messrs Coleman, and developing further inventions of his own, Alfred Yarrow had accumulated a capital of £1000 and decided to open works of his own.

His idea was to secure a business repairing river boats on the Thames until other ideas could be developed, and surely no great engineering firm ever started in a more humble fashion than the Yarrow works.

His partner was a man named Hedley, who possessed no capital but a certain connexion with those using the river which they hoped would bring in the orders. Their works were situated in the Isle of Dogs, and consisted of two old cottages and a few broken-down sheds which adjoined a public-house.

It wasn't exactly the sort of workshop about which an ambitious boy dreams, but Yarrow did not waste time in brooding about their humble start in life. The ground-floor of the two cottages was converted into a store, and the upper floor became a drawing office, while the yard was fitted with shipbuilding tools. Lady Yarrow tells us :

> The great attraction of the place in his eyes was that, being an old repairing shop in which the owner had failed, a few tools remained, and would be rented with the buildings, obviating the need of capital to purchase them. These tools

consisted of a few punching and drilling machines, an old broken-down factory engine and a boiler of 6 horse-power. The tools for the engineer's shop had to be purchased. The yard and buildings covered in all half an acre.

Having erected a signboard bearing the magic inscription

YARROW & HEDLEY

ENGINEERS

they next built an engineer's shop and fitted it with lathes and tools.

Two months later the works were ready, and then began the most anxious period of Yarrow's life. Despite valiant efforts to secure work, and a few small jobs which they did obtain, money was lost during the first year. During that time the average number of men employed was twelve, and expenditure included labour £800, material £1500, overhead charges £600. Thus the total cost of the works amounted to £2900. The amount earned came to £2800, so that Yarrow and his partner had toiled for twelve months, and at the end of it lost £100 of their scanty capital.

That loss was not due to any want of trying. They accepted any and every order that came along. Their first job had been the construction of a burglar-proof door for a safe in a Brighton jeweller's. The next was the erection of an iron roller in Southwark Bridge Road. Then came an order for overhead travelling pans to be fitted up in a sugar factory.

Other early orders included an apparatus for roasting coffee, match-making machinery, the repair of a boiler in a jam factory—many and varied were the jobs which they undertook in a desperate fight for success.

During the second year the partners tried to get bigger orders for more important work, and as a result finished up with a loss of £2000, which meant that their capital was gone and they were in debt.

Something had to be done. Yarrow cast around for an idea which would make the works profitable, and finally decided upon a plan which had been in the back of his mind for many years. This was the building of steam launches similar to one which Yarrow and Hilditch had built years before when engineering was but a hobby. Having decided to build launches, Yarrow inserted an advertisement in several newspapers reading :

> STEAM LAUNCHES.—Anyone wanting a steam launch would be well served if they came to Yarrow & Hedley, Isle of Dogs.

Three days later he booked his first order for a launch with a single-cylinder engine and a vertical boiler of 3 horse-power. The price was to be £145.

The boat took three months to build and cost £200. But although money was lost, it was the turning-point in his fortunes. At the end of the summer Yarrow bought the launch back for £100 and sold her the same day for £200. And realizing that there should be a trade in these vessels, he toured the Thames in the launch, landing at each riverside inn and asking permission to hang photographs of the launch, with details of her builders, in some prominent place.

Orders began to arrive, at first from the Thames valley, and later from shipping companies who wanted launches to be attached to ocean-going liners. For seven years these launches were built without ceasing, no other work being taken.

In 1875 Yarrow built the first of his boats which made history. This was the *Ilala*, destined for Lake Nyassa in Africa, and which became the first British steamer to be launched upon an African waterway.

To get it there the boat had to be built in sections of not more than fifty pounds each, for it had to be man-carried through sixty miles of African jungle to reach the lake. Nothing like this had ever been made before, but that fact only made Yarrow more determined to succeed, and in October 1875 the *Ilala* entered Nyassa, 1400 miles from the sea, there to take up the work of subduing the slave trade in that part of Africa.

Other boats built by Yarrow to assist in this great work were the *Pioneer* and *Adventure*, two gunboats sent in sections through Africa by the British Admiralty to prevent the slaves being conveyed across the lake to the coast.

Thirty-three years after the arrival of the *Ilala*, the last native dhow, full of slaves, was captured on Lake Nyassa, and slavery was practically abolished. There is thus a direct connexion between those first small Yarrow works on the side of the Thames in London and the greater happiness which the suppression of the slave traffic in the 'Livingstone' country had brought to the people of darkest Africa.

Success had now come to Yarrow, success which the breaking of the partnership with Hedley did not diminish. A wonderful reputation for good work and modern developments had been built up in the expanding works at Poplar, and Yarrow found himself free of financial worries and able to devote his whole time to research in those lines of marine engineering and shipbuilding which interested him most.

Launches were built and sent to all parts of the globe. When the torpedo came, Alfred Yarrow perfected a system for discharging them, a development which may have first turned his attention to the construction of torpedo-boats.

The first torpedo-boats built at the Yarrow works were ordered by the Argentine Government, and were little more than the famous Yarrow launches adapted for the special work they were intended to do.

Between 1877 and 1879 orders for the high-speed vessels which Yarrow had now developed, and which were particularly suited for torpedo work, came to the firm from the Argentine, Dutch, French, Russian, Greek, Spanish, Austrian, Italian, and Chilian Governments.

About this time the British Admiralty ordered a number of 'sample' high-speed boats. The orders were given to firms which were considered to offer a reasonable prospect of carrying out the work successfully, and among these was the firm of Yarrow. The contract necessitated the building of a torpedo-boat which would attain a speed of 18 knots, then believed to be the highest speed attainable by a naval vessel.

Of the various shipbuilders who entered the competition, the boat built by Alfred Yarrow gave the best performance, attaining a speed of nearly 22 knots during her trials, or 2½ knots ahead of the highest speed attained by any of the other vessels tested under similar conditions.

Later, two torpedo-boats originally built for Russia, but later taken over by the British Government, took part in a big naval review in the Solent, when their speed of 21 knots astonished the assembled notabilities and experts. With the public performance of these two vessels, Yarrow's name as a builder of high-speed craft was brought before the public for the first time.

Other notable high-speed vessels which Alfred Yarrow built during the years that followed included the *Batoom,* a torpedo-boat 100 feet long, with a speed of 22 knots, which was constructed for Russia and made the journey from the Thames to the Black Sea safely, and the *Hornet,* built in 1892 for the British Navy.

The *Hornet* was the first torpedo-boat destroyer ever built. She came into being because Alfred Yarrow, having built the fastest torpedo-boats in the world, realized the need of still faster ships which could, in case of war, hunt down the torpedo-boats. Admiral Sir John Fisher, then Controller of the Navy, upon learning of the exceptionally fast torpedo-boats then being built for the French Navy, ordered Yarrow to produce a new class of boat which would be the fastest craft afloat.

The result was the *Hornet* and her sister ship, the *Havock,* 180 feet long and driven by engines of 4000 horse-power. On their official trials, the *Hornet* attained a speed of 27·3 knots and the *Havock* 26·1 knots. The difference in their speeds was due to the fact that the former ship was fitted with Yarrow water-tube boilers, which proved superior to the older type of locomotive boiler used in the sister vessel.

As a result of the speed of these ships, especially in rough water, the modern torpedo-boat destroyer came into being and has since been added to every navy, while the superior speed of the *Hornet* led to the Yarrow boiler being introduced into the British Navy.

Passing from success to success—and still specializing in high-speed boats all the time—Alfred Yarrow soon

THE YARROW-HILDITCH STEAM CARRIAGE

eclipsed his own record by building the first destroyer to attain a speed of 30 knots.

This was the *Sokol*, built for the Russian Government. In it Yarrow used high-tensile steel for the first time; this reduced the weight of metal necessary for safety and assisted him in his task of securing greater speed. The success resulted in high-tensile steel being exclusively used in the construction of similar vessels throughout the world, and its discovery was due to the man who might have spent his life as the partner of an obscure firm of agricultural engineers but for a lucky chance of fate.

But all these performances were eclipsed by three super-destroyers which Alfred Yarrow built for the British Government a year or two before the World War. For months the great shipbuilder had been warning the Admiralty that Germany was building 30-knot destroyers which could outpace the 27-knot boats which were still being built in this country, and at last the Admiralty placed an order with Yarrow for three fast destroyers.

The result was the building of the *Lurcher*, which developed a speed of over 35 knots, or almost exactly double the speed demanded and expected by the British Admiralty when holding its first competition for torpedo-boats years earlier.

When in the spring of 1912 a race was organized between the various types of high-speed ships in the Fleet, the Yarrow-built destroyer which competed left her opponent five miles behind in a race of two hours' duration.

We have not the space here to relate the equally romantic story of the development of the Yarrow boiler which played such a prominent part in these high-speed triumphs, and which has been fitted to warships in all the navies in the world.

In the construction of high-speed vessels, and in marine boiler development, Alfred Yarrow has led the way for half a century—ever since, indeed, the day, when spurred on by the necessity of saving his works from bankruptcy, he inserted that advertisement in the Press offering to build launches for pleasure-seekers on the Thames. One thing can be said with confidence—if Alfred Yarrow and his half-acre workshop had failed during those days of crisis, neither British nor German warships would have attained the speeds which were achieved during the War. Those speeds were made possible almost entirely by the genius of this one pioneer.

When, in the early years of this century, Alfred Yarrow decided to remove the works which had grown out of the original two cottages and collection of sheds to be one of the biggest on the Thames, over four hundred invitations reached him from mayors, town councillors, chairmen of dock boards, and others, all anxious to secure the great Yarrow works for their city or port.

The move was made because Yarrow realized that shipbuilding was a declining industry in the South, and the complete disappearance of the industry on the Thames since that time proves that Sir Alfred Yarrow was right. The site selected for the new works was on the Clyde, in the heart of the greatest shipbuilding yards in the world. Between 4000 and 5000 tons of material had to be transported, which included everything from the most delicate models to the heaviest machine tools. Everything was taken by rail, and when the move was in full swing, a train-load of from forty to fifty wagons left the works at Poplar every day. On July 14, 1908, the first destroyer was launched from the new works at Scotstoun.

During the Great War these works were employed day and night building the high-speed boats which helped to destroy the German submarines and protect our food ships. Improvement after improvement was made by Yarrow, until he built his final triumph, the *Tyrian*, which achieved within a fraction of 40 knots the greatest speed achieved by any ships on active service before 1918. Nor did Sir Alfred Yarrow content himself with building the fastest destroyers in the world, and building as many of them as he could. Several minor inventions which he produced were taken up by the authorities, including the 'Miranda' life-saving waistcoat, so designed that it could be worn constantly without interfering with the wearer's freedom of movement as would the ordinary life-belt.

In May 1922 this remarkable man, whose life-story is one of the greatest romances in the history of industry, was formally elected a Fellow of the Royal Society, suitable honour to crown a life spent in research and invention which began with the automatic wool-winder invented at the age of eight and ended, so far as actual invention is concerned, with those 40-knot destroyers which were the pride of the British Navy and the protection of our coasts during the war.

Perhaps because of the memory of his own difficulties in early years, Sir Alfred Yarrow has always taken the greatest interest in young men who, as he once did, face the beginning of their careers, and he has given away much of the money which his success has brought him in an effort to make their path easier. Especially his personal experience of the difficulties of conducting research work when worried about finance impressed itself upon his mind, and in 1923 he presented the Royal Society with £100,000, the income to be used to enable a certain number of distinguished scientific men to conduct their studies without financial worry.

Since Sir Alfred Yarrow made his first launch the world has speeded up on land and sea. And hitherto unheard-of speeds have been achieved in the air. It is appropriate, therefore, that this volume which records the stories of many of the most remarkable men of our time should end with the career of a man who can to-day, at eighty-six years of age, look back upon a lifetime devoted to the development of speed on the sea, a lifetime which, but for an accident to a mounted policeman in his youth, might have been devoted to speed on land. For if the Yarrow steam carriage had not been prohibited except when preceded by a man carrying a red flag, its inventor might easily have become the first of the great motor-car manufacturers. And in that case our destroyers might not have attained 40 knots on the high seas, and Henry Ford might not have had the opportunity of developing the popular car before anyone else thought of it.